Armin Mueller-Stahl

ARMIN MUELLER-STAHL

Rockets to the Moon

An Anti-Arms Picture-Book

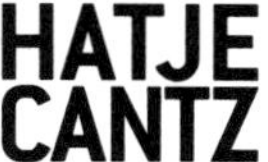

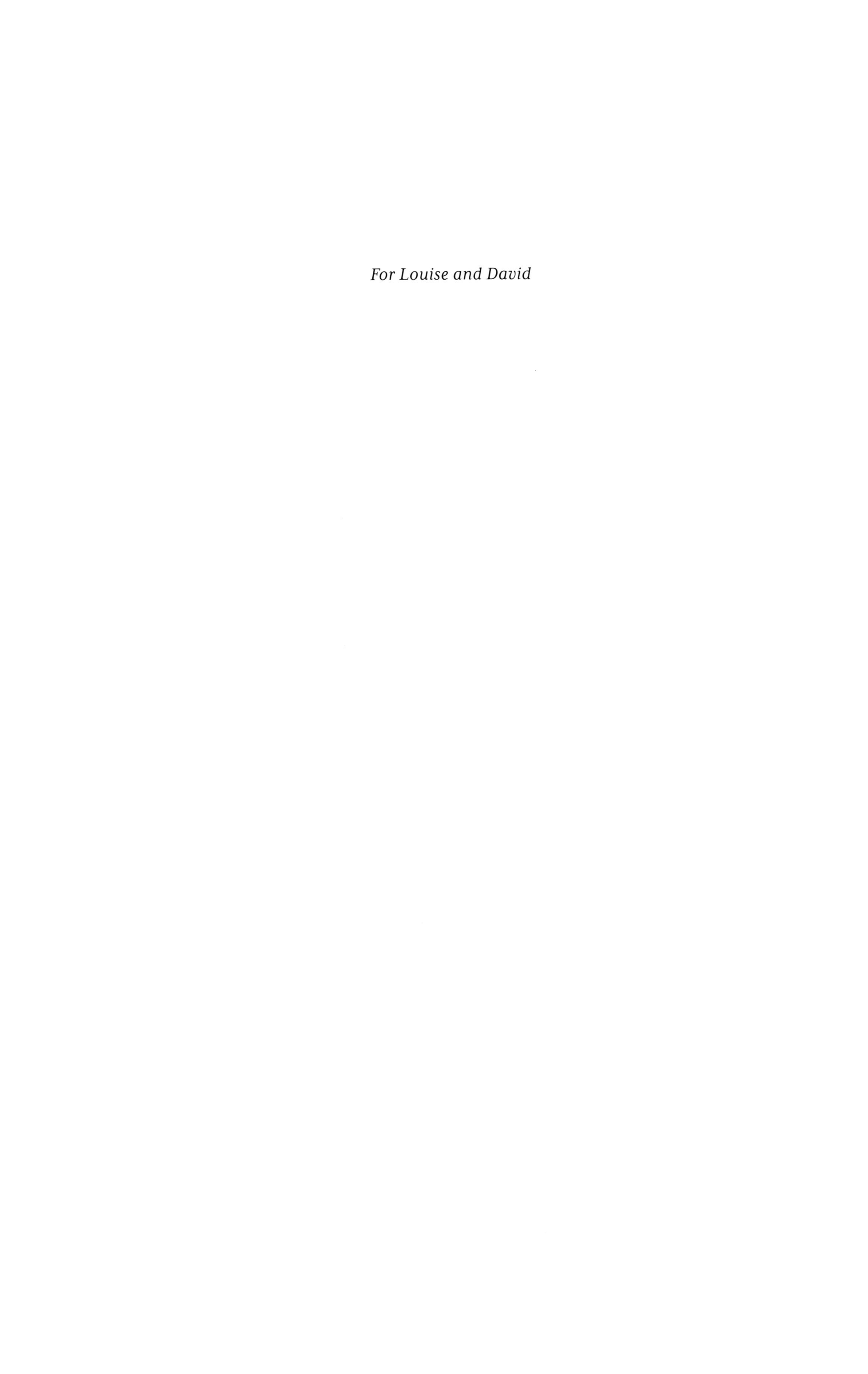

For Louise and David

Contents

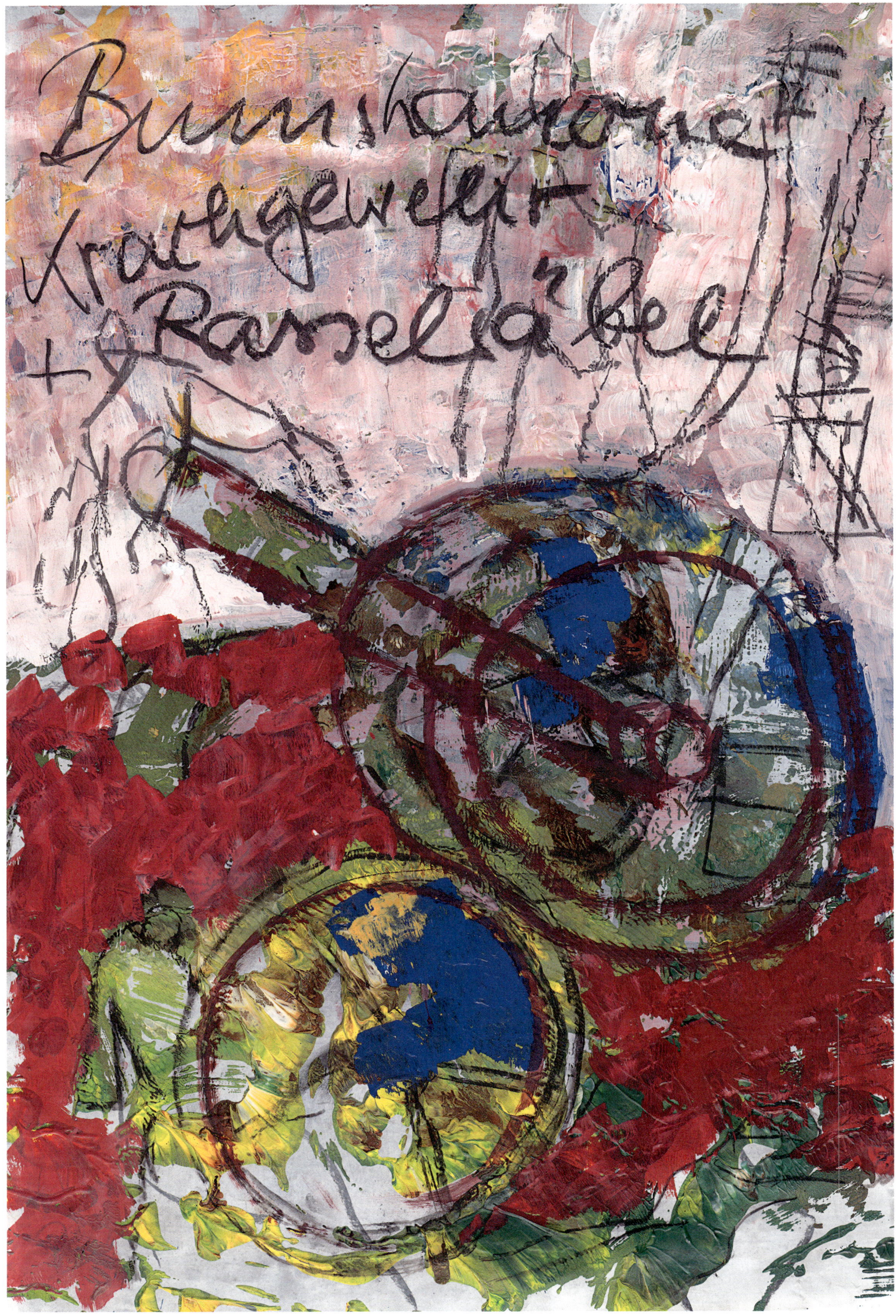

A *Citoyen* – In Lieu of a Foreword

He said it straight and tall / We have citizens' joy / Achieved by means of a Wall (From *Walter U.*, 1961); *There once was a blue cow / She drank herself quite out / She was really wasted, she was quite empty / Now no bigger than a louse* (From *Es war mal eine blaue Kuh [There Once Was a Blue Cow]*, 1964); *The Stasi came to fetch the soup / To cook it anew according to party line, but hush! / They cooked what? A stinking mush* (From *Columbus 64 [Film with Ulrich Thein]*, 1966); *Over the wall, he headed out / To escape the will of the State / Once in a while, there is a man / Who'll soar like a bird to seal his fate* (From *Der wien Vogel fliegen kann [He Who Can Fly Like a Bird]*, 1968); *Of course they were the Stasi / With nose, and ears, full face / Three of them still there / Molochs sniffing all over the place* (From *Marie hat eine Nase [Marie Has a Nose]*, 1976); *Hey, our national court / Muted tongues / Soon we'll sit in jail / And scratch our bellies / No hope of bail!* (From *Neue Gesetze 1. Aug 1979 [New Laws 1st Aug 1979]*, 1979)

And now "Rockets to the Moon," an anti-armament poem, written as early as 1964, to which a postscript was added in 2018: *With the weapons / Giddyup / The rockets at the dump / The weapons' lobby a new lease / Heavenly peace . . .*

Not for the first time when signing the petition protesting stripping Wolf Biermann of his East German citizenship in 1976, but long before that—and up to the present—Armin Mueller-Stahl has revealed himself to be a self-confident and unbending political person, an artist who thinks, works, and lives in the spirit of the Enlightenment, who never sought to be one thing: a citizen with the blessing of a state or party.

His resistance to nannying, oppression, and inhumanity, born and grown out of his experience, his intellectual insight, and his unwavering faith in the dignity of all human beings, who cannot be allowed to fall victim to any system, ideology, or party, is a thread that runs through his life and determines his thinking even today—and finds expression in his entire creative activity: in songs, poems, essays, novels, interviews, in stage and film roles, and in these painted "images of human beings."

"Lieber einen Knick in der Karriere als im Rückgrat" (Better a kink in your career than in your backbone), he said once. To remain true to such a maxim, as both history and the present teach us, is bitterly difficult. Mueller-Stahl has remained faithful to it. Respect!

Björn Engholm, Lübeck

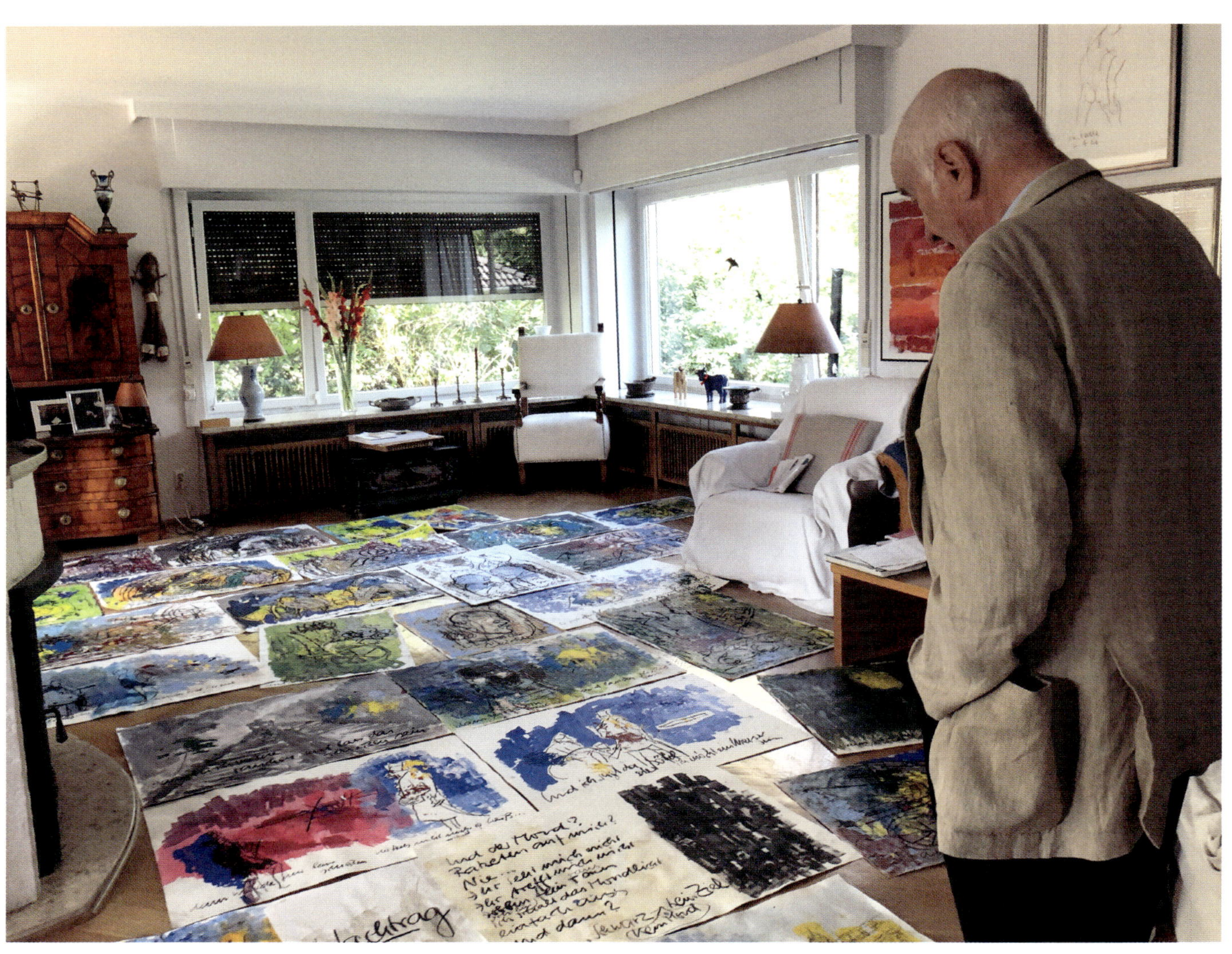

The Silence of the Weapons

Silence—he experienced it once, back then, in Prenzlau: "I'm listening, and I hear nothing. That was: peace," is how Armin Mueller-Stahl tells it. End of the war in Europe. Silence as a precondition for something new beginning. Musician, actor, and lecturers have to be able to endure silence as well. In silence, in hesitating before a play, in play with and playing on, when one doesn't "have a text" oneself right then, in the general pause. A piece of music has to be able to breathe out after the last note, a drama after its last line. Don't applaud right away! First feel what has ended, just two, three briefest moments, one inhalation long, perhaps.

Apropos inhalation: Volksbühne Berlin, 1964, Armin Mueller-Stahl is playing Mercutio in *Romeo and Juliet*. Tybalt stabs Mercutio on the balcony; Mercutio falls, plunges, rolls down thirty-two steps. At the foot of the stairs, he has to remain lying there for three or four minutes until the next curtain. Dead, of course. But after the rehearsed duel and the fall, his heart and breathing are racing. Silent, staccato breathing, as shallowly and quickly as possible, was his solution. What strain, what work— rehearsing his art to the point of artistic mastery, and the better the actor becomes, the less the audience notices it.

Armin Mueller-Stahl learned early on that life can turn suddenly at any minute in a grotesque-cruel way and suddenly tumble away. On May 1, 1945, his father died in a military hospital in Mecklenburg. His medical file was never found. For that reason, Mueller-Stahl believes that his father had been shot as a deserter by military police. His family learned about his father's death nearly thirty years later.

But on that same May 1, 1945, a Red Army soldier threatened to shoot fourteen-year-old Armin Mueller-Stahl. Because he thought he belonged to the Hitler Youth. He shouted at him in Russian, pushing him against the wall of a barn. At the last second, a Pole who had just been released by from captivity as a prisoner of war of the Germans knocked the soldier's gun away. Or did he rather fall to his knee and beg for Armin's life and his own? Mueller-Stahl no longer knows, only that he then ran away.

Aus dem Leben eines Gauklers (From the Life of a Troubadour) was the name of the evening just under twenty years ago when Mueller-Stahl told that story as part of the *Berliner Lektionen* (Berlin Readings). One inevitably thinks of Chaplin's *The Great Dictator*: the poor barber in the ghetto is threatened by a Nazi mob; the rope is around his neck; they are already pulling him up on the lamppost—a high-ranking Nazi interrupts the lynching. The two men recognize each other; the high-ranking Nazi owes his life to the Jew, who asks the Nazi: "Well, how are you?"

Of the many honors bestowed on the actor Armin Mueller-Stahl, the Chaplin

Shoe, which has long since ceased to be conferred, is by no means the least appropriate. Chaplin, too, was talented in music, often composing and conducting his own soundtracks. Also because Mueller-Stahl has mastered slapstick more than is generally known. On East German television, he did farce and stand-up comedy—very popular, very successful. Chaplin and Mueller-Stahl are also linked by an unerring sense of balance, for an equilibrist's wobbling. The roller-skating scene in *Modern Times*? With a blindfold over his eyes, Charlie skates along the edge. When he removes the blindfold, he starts to thrash his skates back and forth in a panic, as if he is trying to get away from the abyss but cannot, as if in a bad dream, but only for a moment. Before it becomes too much, it is already over. The immortal episode in the yellow New York taxi in Jim Jarmusch's *Night on Earth*: Mueller-Stahl is Helmut; he used to be a circus clown in East Germany, playing two flutes at the same time. Yo Yo, his passenger, who has taken over the wheel of the automatic car from the helpless taxi driver laughs himself silly. Both of them are wearing those fur-lined winter caps with ear flaps that fly up and down like a beagle's ears. Yo Yo's is the dernier cri, and has nothing to do with Helmut's widget. And in general: "Helmet? That's like naming your kid Lampshade." And the inherent joke: lampshades can indeed have something helmet-like about them. But the way in which Mueller-Stahl as Helmut, after Yo Yo and his sister-in-law are back out of the taxi, stoically and impassively crosses a dark and unfamiliar Brooklyn: the prolonging of the sudden silence is uproarious comedy.

Armin Mueller-Stahl is a master at keeping the in-between in balance.

Until the war and his father's conscription, his home in Tilsit had been an artistic one. His father was a banker but would have preferred to be on stage; he performed in the city's theater as often as he could, wrote sketches for family celebrations, and performed them. The family painted and played music together; his mother's family moved to Prenzlau in 1938; his mother moved out into the countryside to avoid the bombing of the war, but as soon as the war ended, she returned to burned-out Prenzlau. Mueller-Stahl's side talents had begun at home in Tilsit: painting, drawing, music.

Later, as a music student in Berlin, on a path to becoming a professional violinist, he heard Yehudi Menuhin performing under Sergiu Celibidache in the West and his own great role model, David Oistrakh, in the East. Mueller-Stahl certainly knows the recording of Oistrakh and Menuhin performing Bach's Double Violin Concerto in D Minor, BWV 1043, in which, in the simply heavenly Largo, a certain passage occurs: both violin parts have a minimal pause—silence—but the tension is held, until the delicate net of sounds has caught its breath and rises again.

And then the paintings that go with the song that the weapons want to silence. Is the golden king looking at the sky on the "cover" reminiscent of something specific? In the drawing about the "museum of weapons," a thick-nosed Hitler with the blackest mini moustache. Kid-friendly, bright colors cover the weapons, for which thinly rendered stick hands are grabbing; the grenades are filled with the primary colors red, yellow, and blue. The weapons have rusted; the hobbling, onomatopoetic children's verses make them seem a little gaga, but they are indeed cogent in the end. As hammy showing off, the weapons boast about themselves on the scrap pile of history, and the view of the moon opens up a new

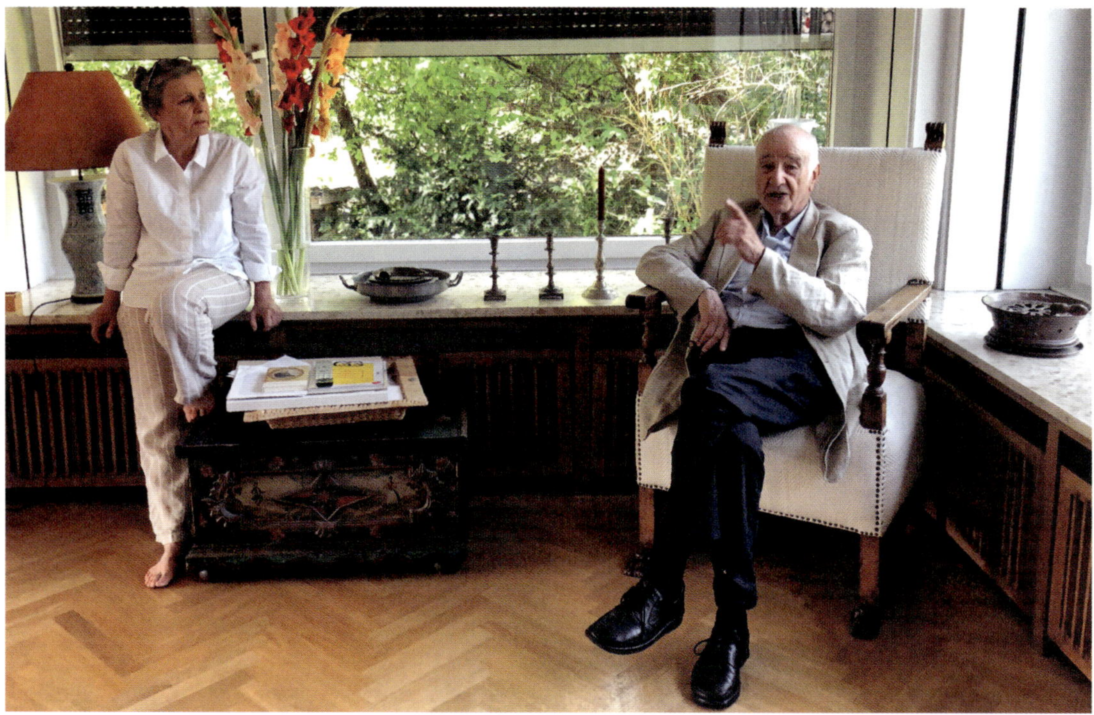

perspective. But first comes the confession, the admission—with a transformation of the cannons into a train, the rifle into an auto, and the saber into a kitchen knife—a forgiveness of sins. The good moon, moving so quietly, distances itself in the postlude—as so often—and turns the main switch off. So the "heavenly peace" descends into the golden final shot like a heavenly Jerusalem. The silence is victorious over the rattle of weapons.

How much talent a single man needs to perform very serious concerts as a violinist, to shine as an actor for six decades, in East and West Germany and internationally; to be able to write and create an oeuvre of paintings of great substance and considerable graphic modernity—and all simultaneously—is not easy to measure. Armin Mueller-Stahl surely numbers among the very rare "multitalents": everything they come across, they can recast as art. And it is inspiring and admirable how consistent he remains in his work of artistic transformation. For sixty years, he says he was the troubadour, the tragedian, and the fool—so he presents it

in his poem, or couplet, "Der Gaukler" (The Troubadour). How many people did he alone offer in that way a profound and heartening joy! Beautiful and enchanting, and we see here that it is not yet by any means over.

Philipp Hontschik

Rockets to the Moon

Once there were three weapons
Just rattling around
Deep in a darkened corner
In the museum in town

It was the rattling saber
Plus an old grenade one heard
And a large booming cannon
Who all put in a word

And they rattled on and on
And bragged so puffed with air
But shortly afterwards
They confessed—of sins aware

Bragging

Oh said the cannon proud
I needed only once to boom
And with only one large cannonball
Ten regiments met their doom

O said the rifle
I too was proud of dupes
I shot peng full of holes
The city and its troops

Hey returned the saber
With one fell swoop did I
Mow down the king and with one strike
Several heads did fly

Then all the three fell silent
In the mild evening light
If only the rockets there
Had been shot at the moon so bright

Confession

O said the cannon proud
I wish I were a train
Then I would smoke away up front
And halt my shooting brain

Or an auto I would like to be
Said the rifle then I'd know
That when I'd be a' shooting
My neck wouldn't hurt me so

And I said the saber
I'd like to be a knife
I'd cut some ham and bread and apples
And be happy with my life

Then all the three fell silent
In the mild evening light
If only the rockets there
Had been shot at the moon so bright

Postscript

And the moon?
Rockets at me? Are you all nuts?
You see me not
You can't hit me
I am off the hook
I'll just turn off my light
And then no moon no goal nada

P.S.
With the weapons
Giddyup
The rockets at the dump
The weapons' lobby a new lease
Heavenly peace . . .

Text by Armin Mueller-Stahl
(Lyrics from 1964, revised 2018-20)
English translation by Barbara Zeisl Schoenberg

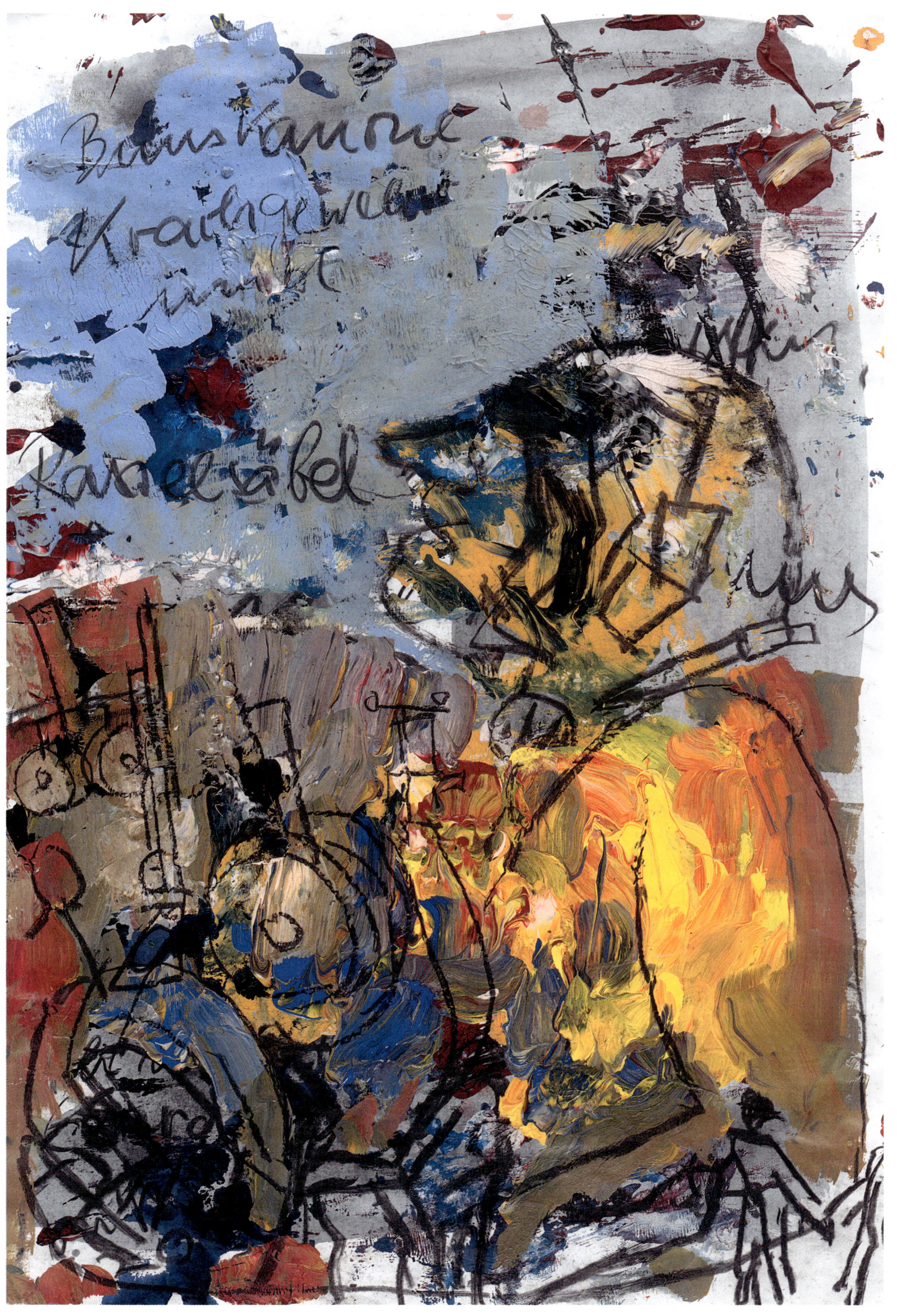
Bahustaume
Kvachgewehre
fürt
Kameefabel

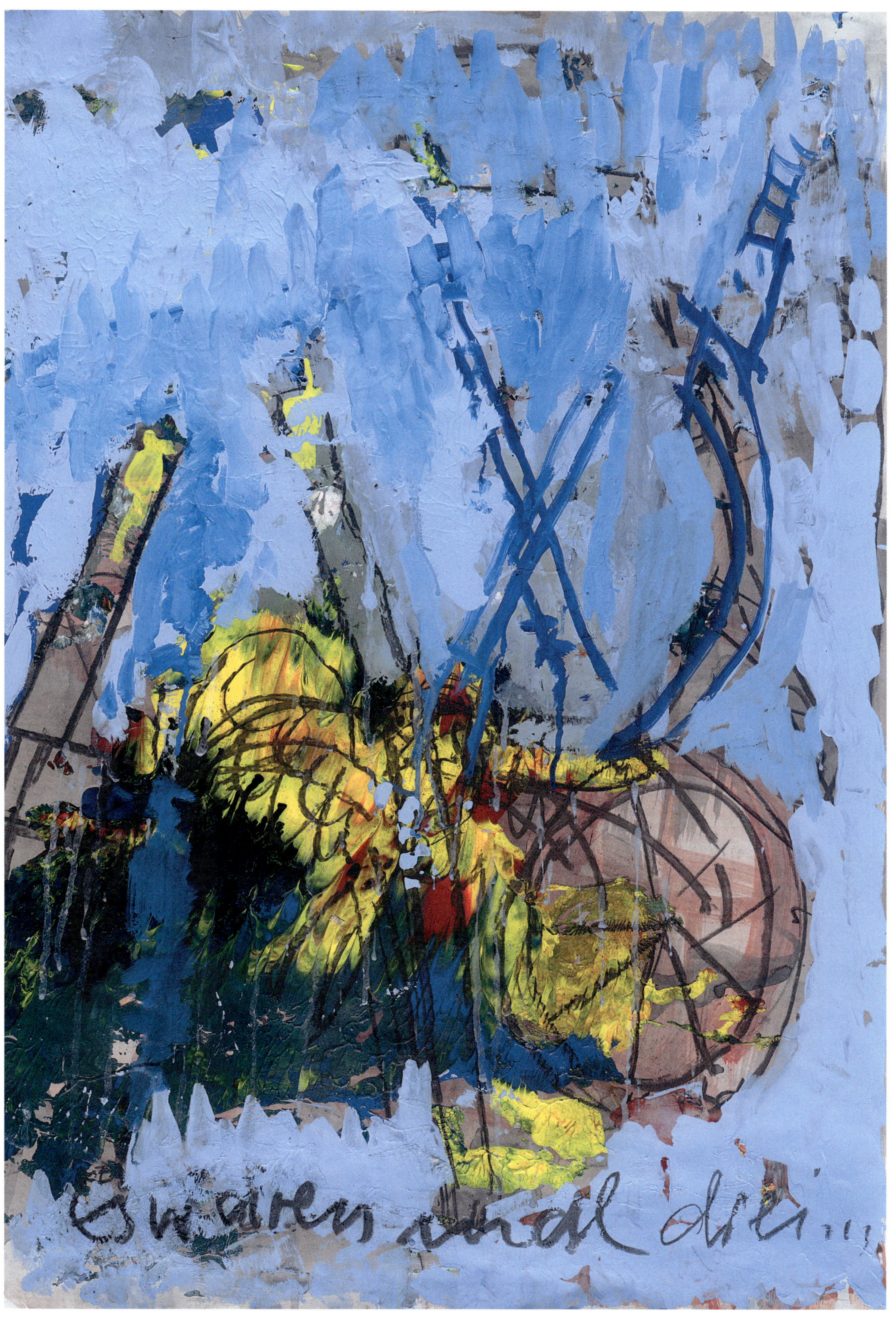
waren und die

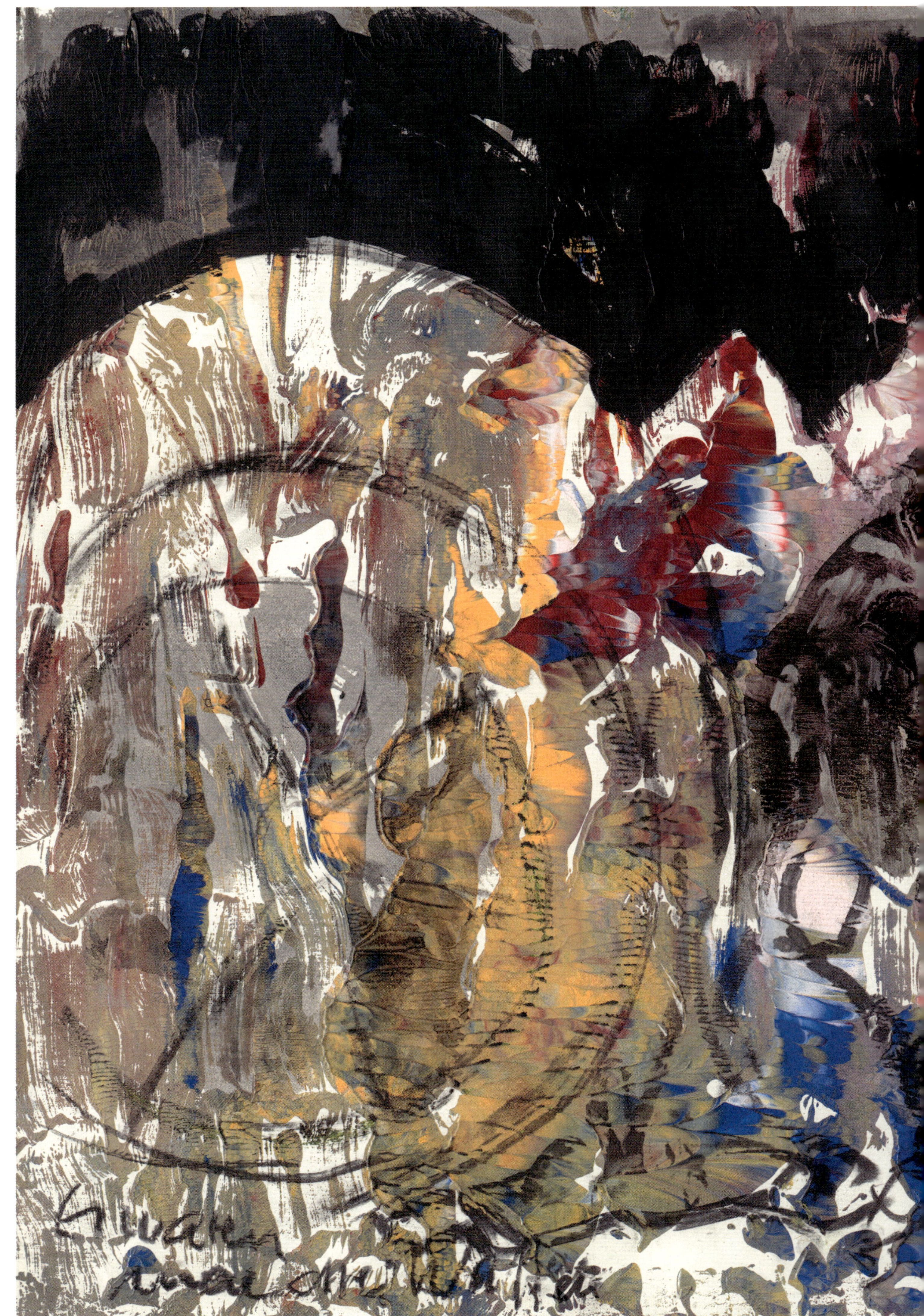

Just rattling around

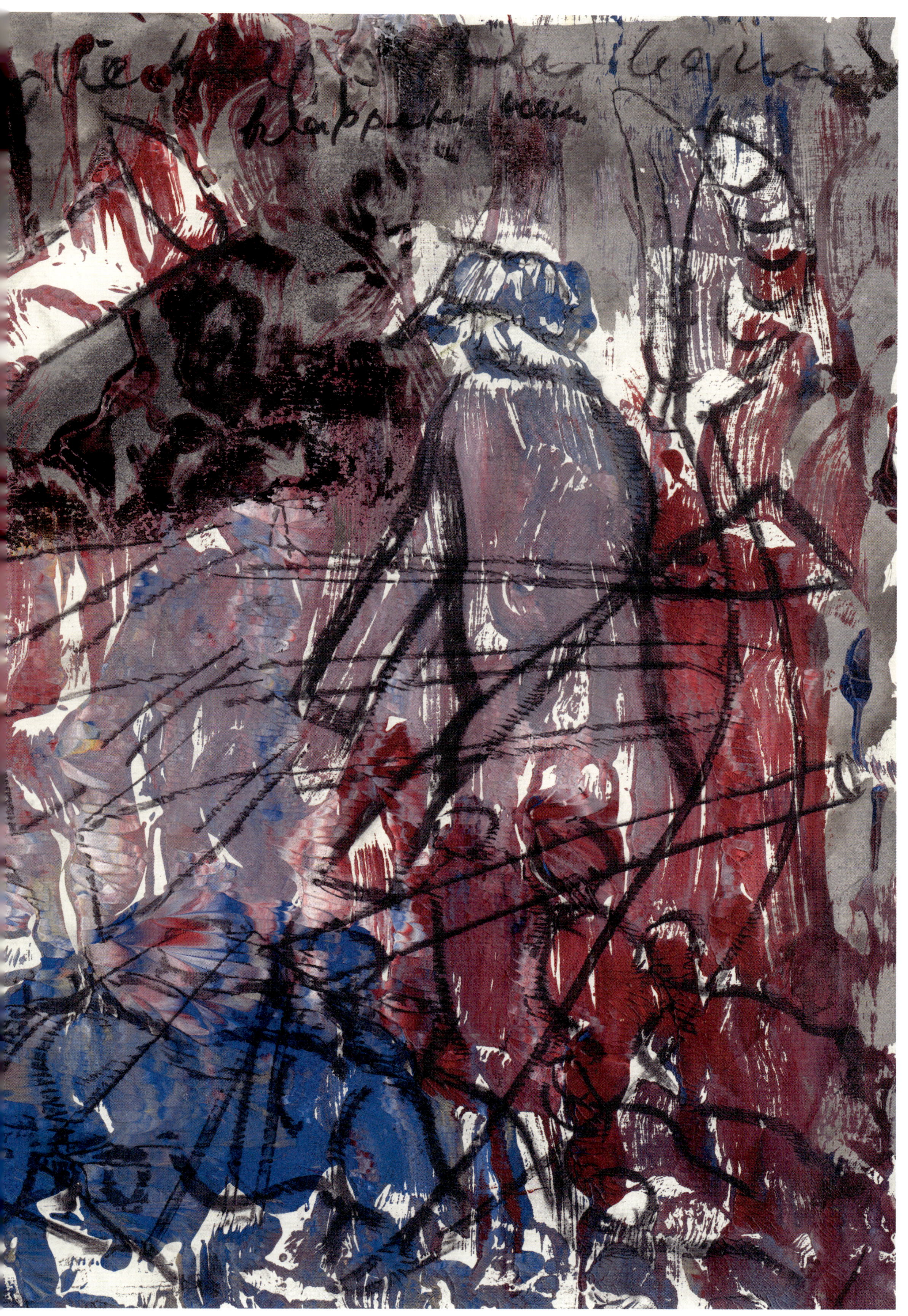

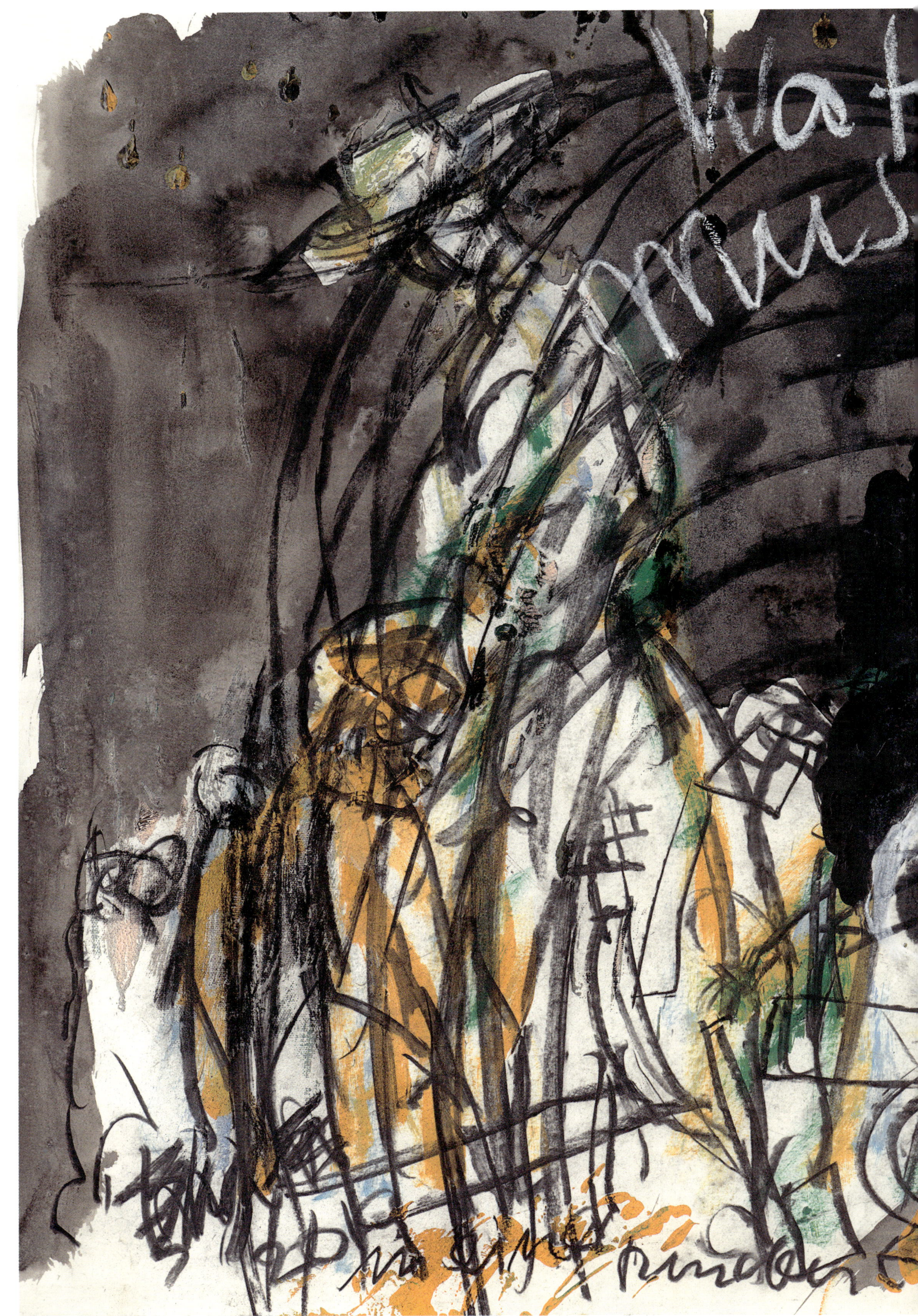

Deep in a darkened corner / In the museum in town

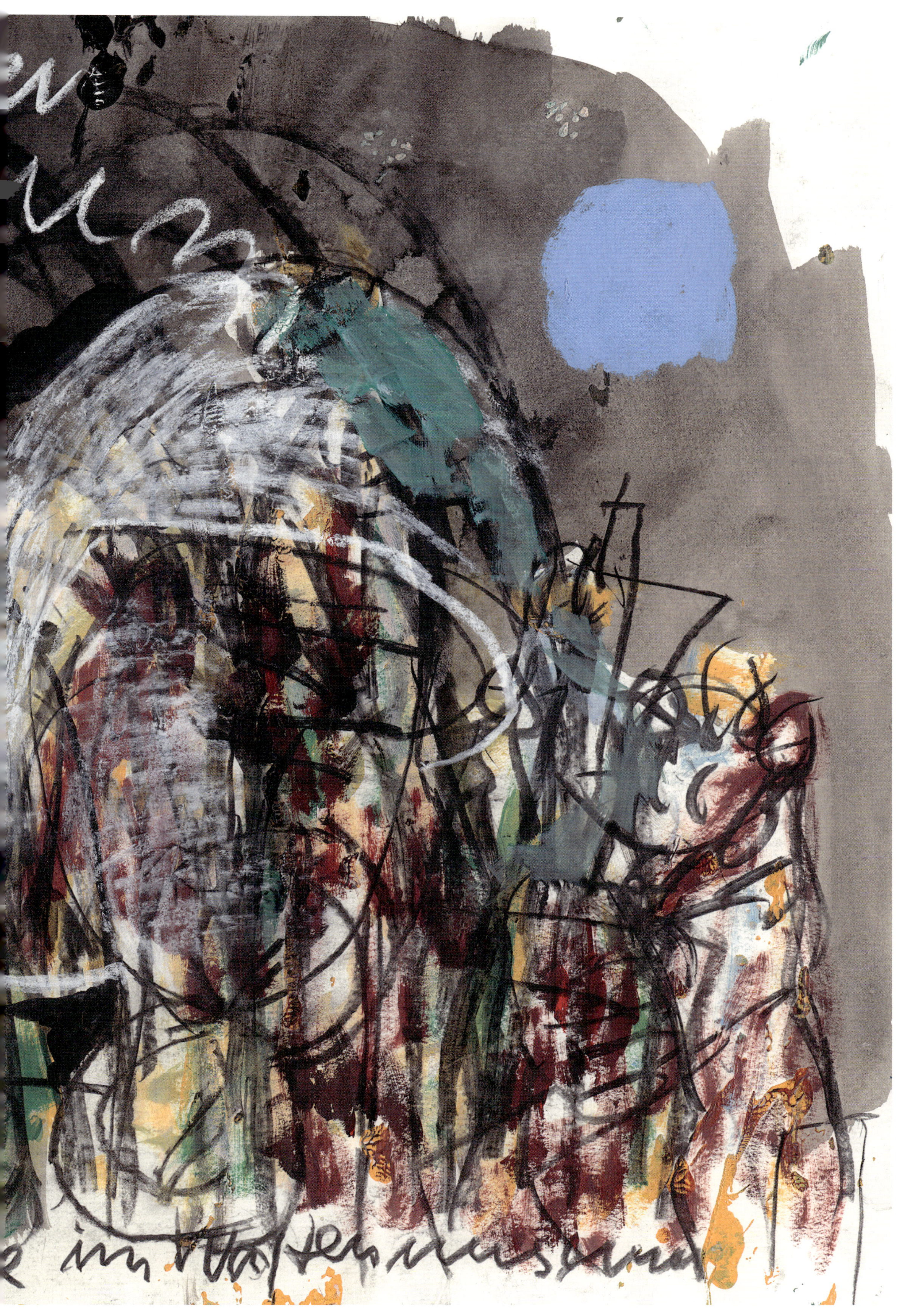

It was the rattling saber

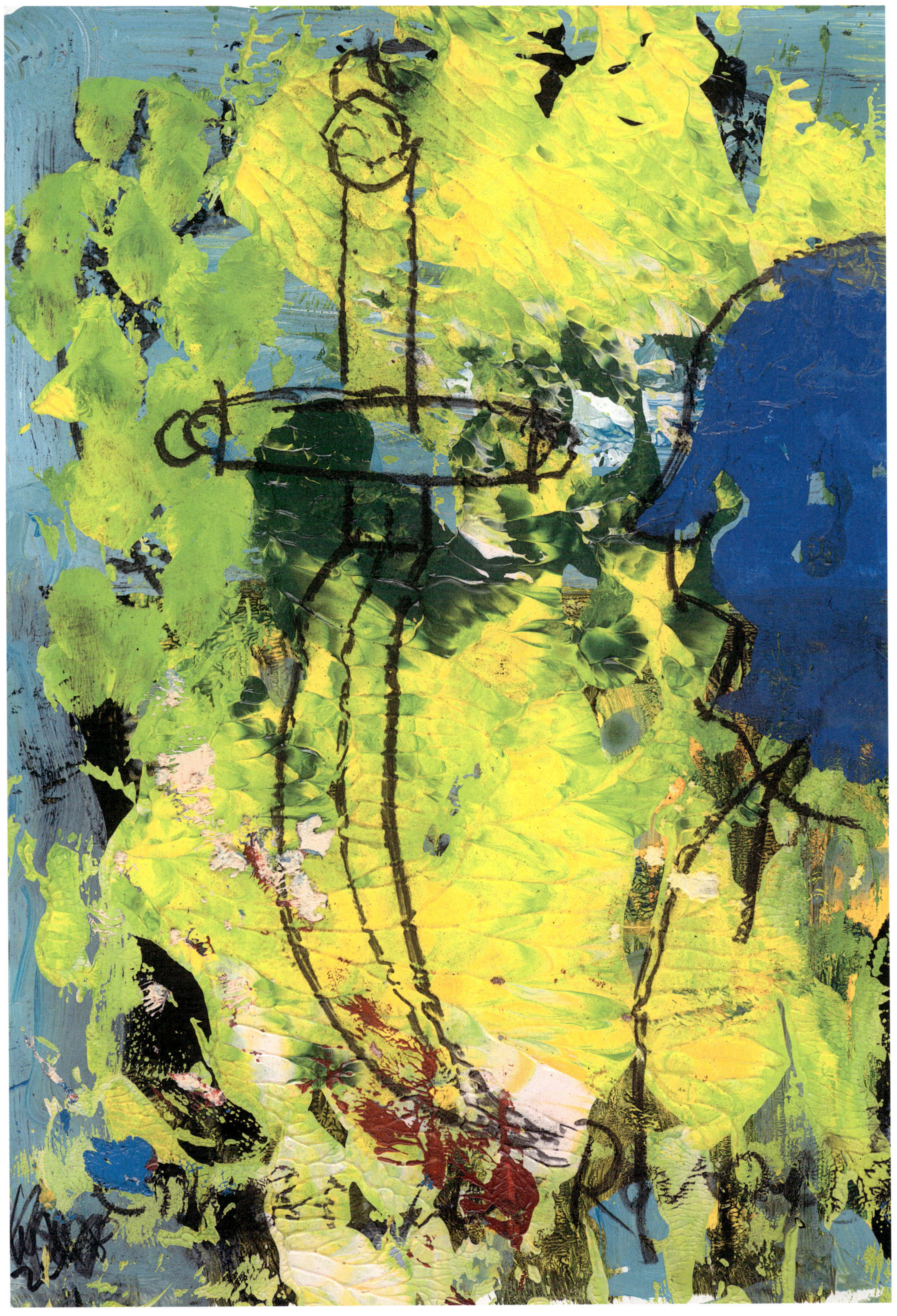

Plus an old grenade one heard

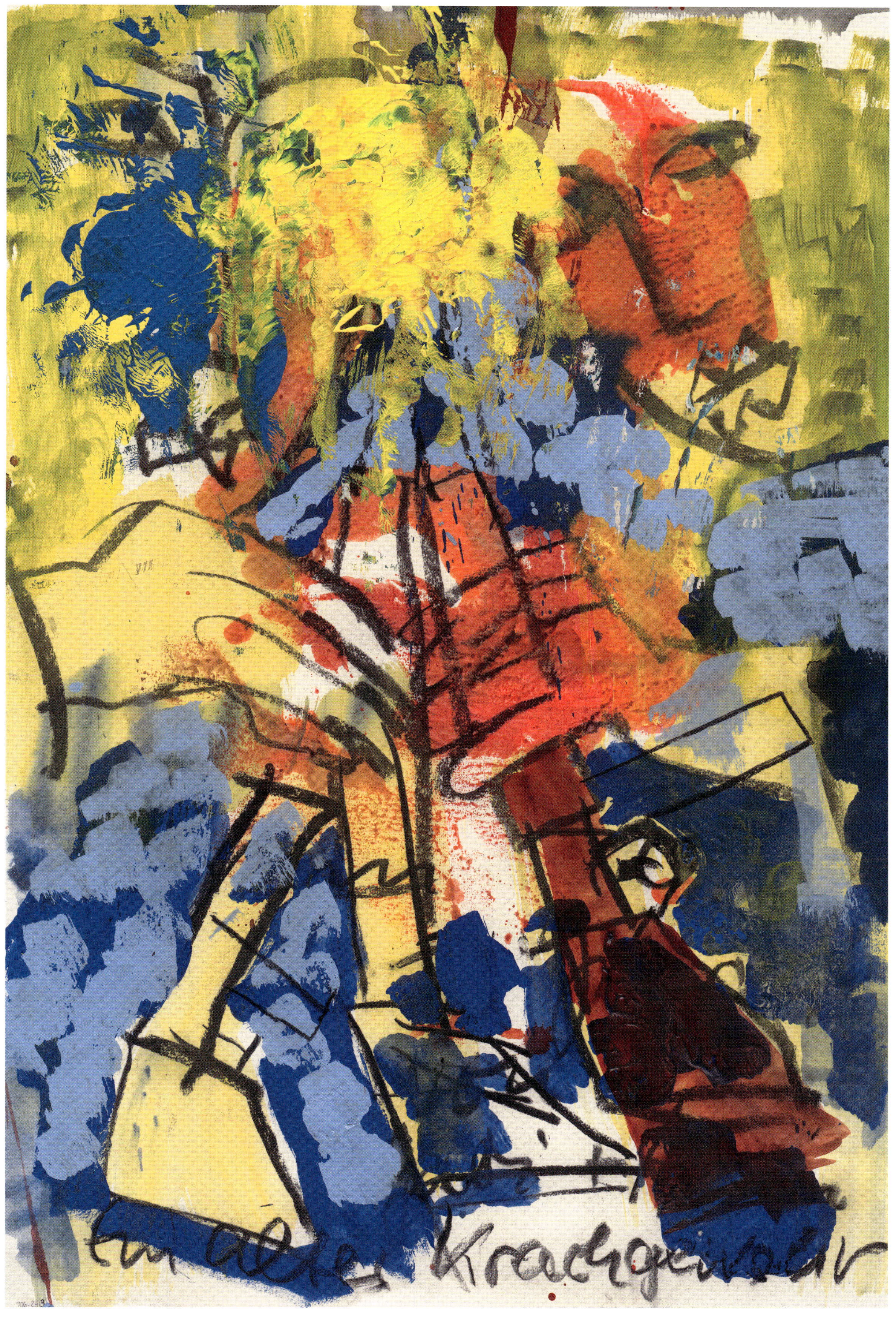
ein alter Krachgeiniar

And a large booming cannon

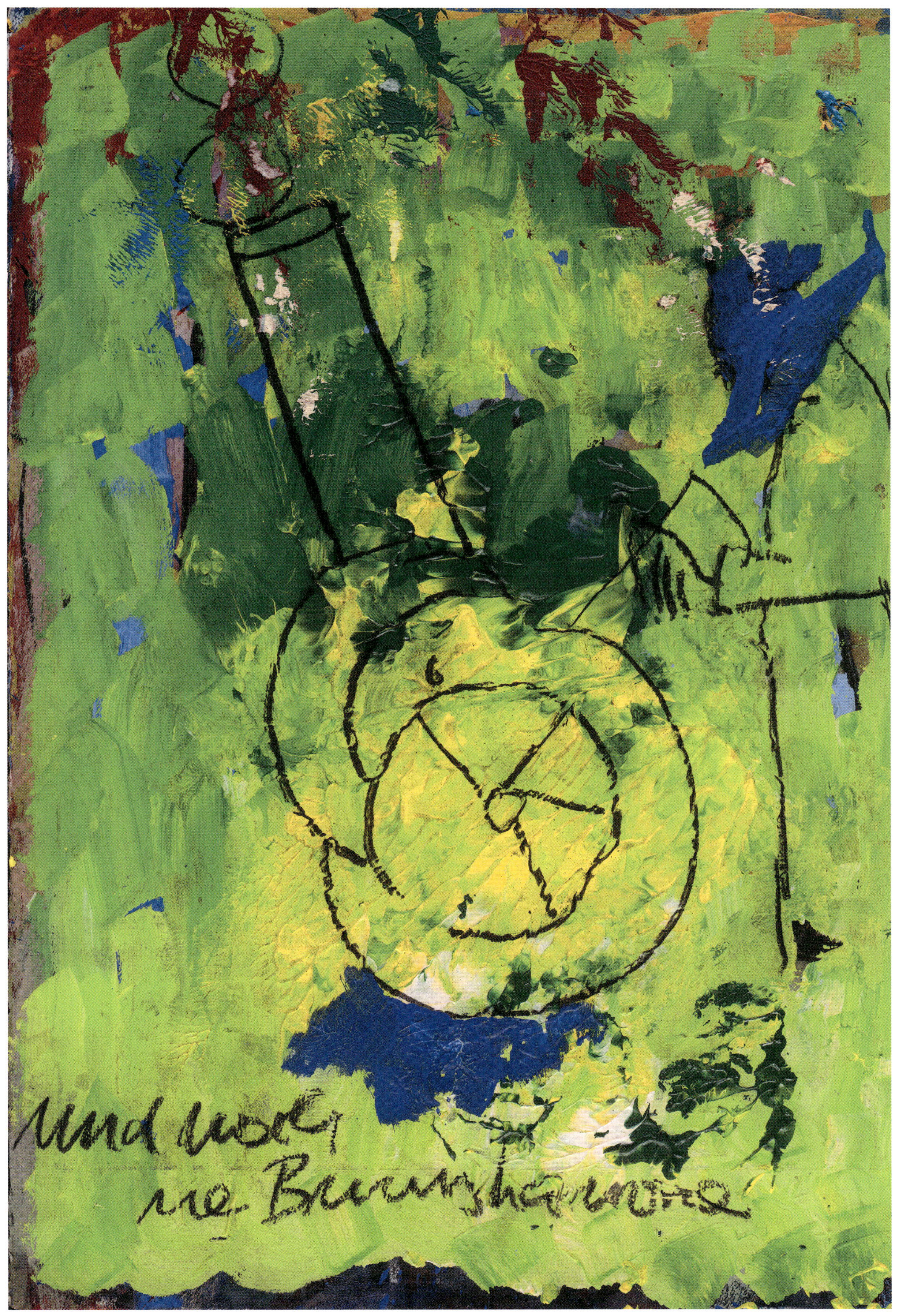

und wie
no Brunnhauma

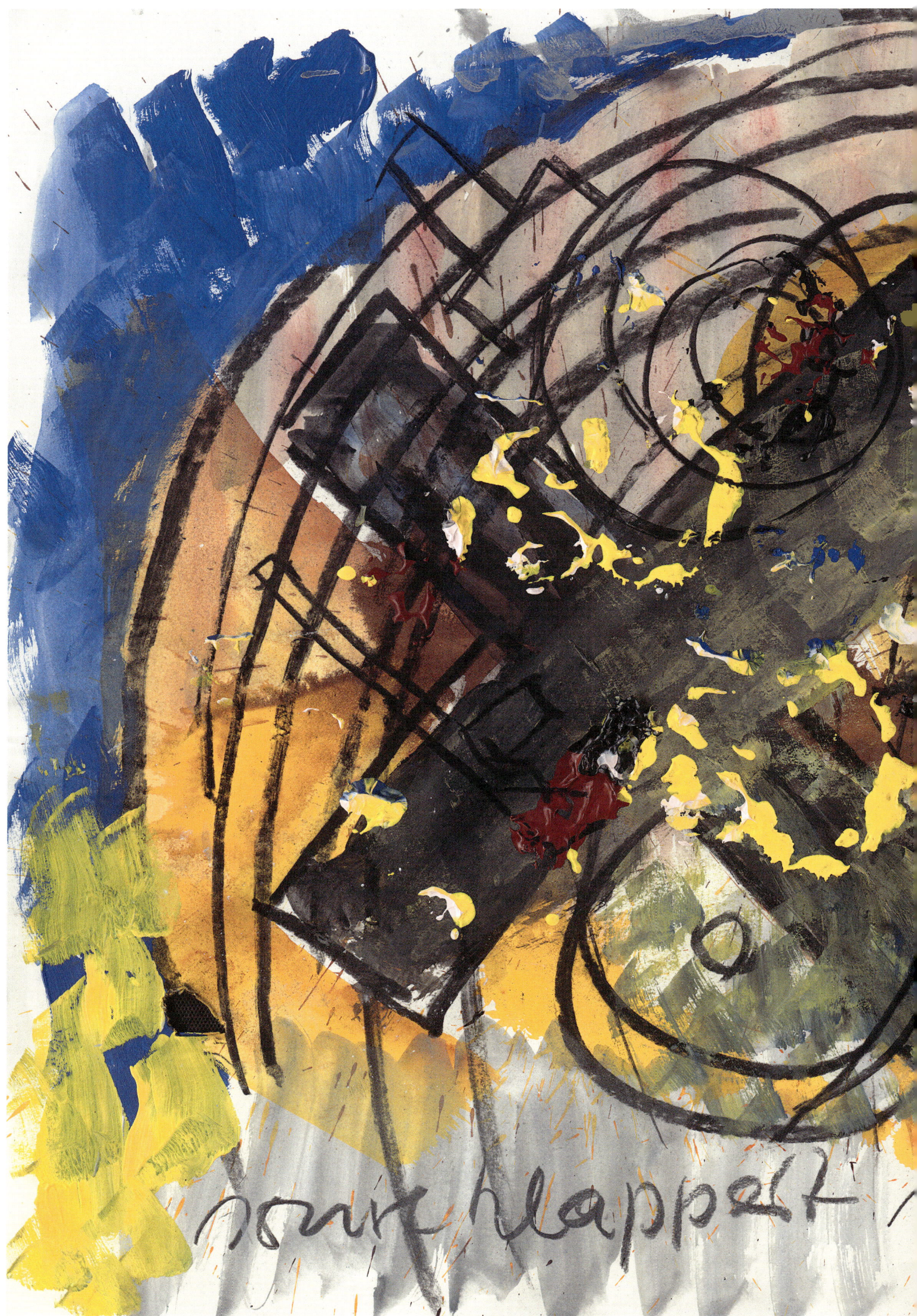

Who all put in a word

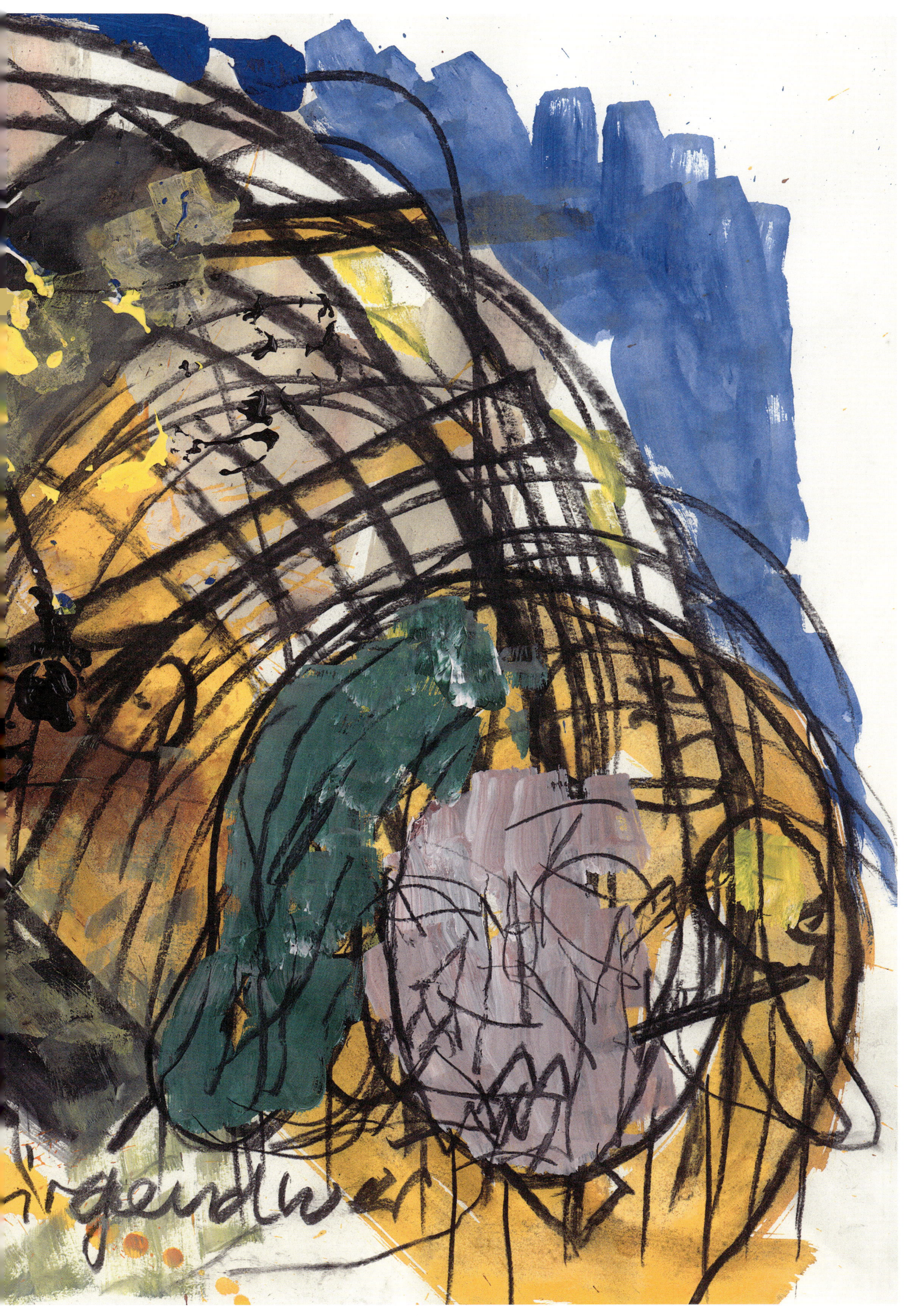

irgendwo

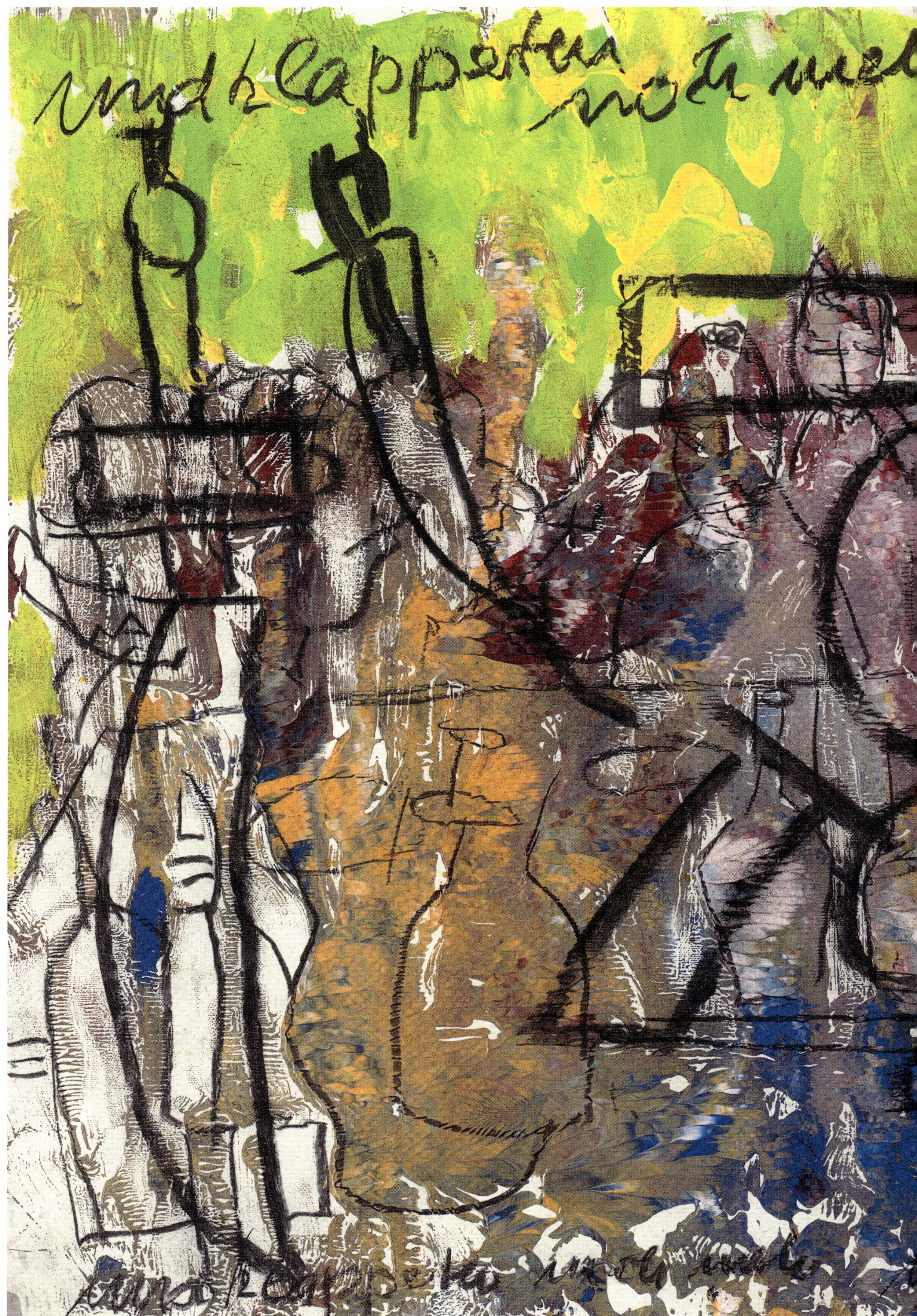

And they rattled on and on / And bragged so puffed with air

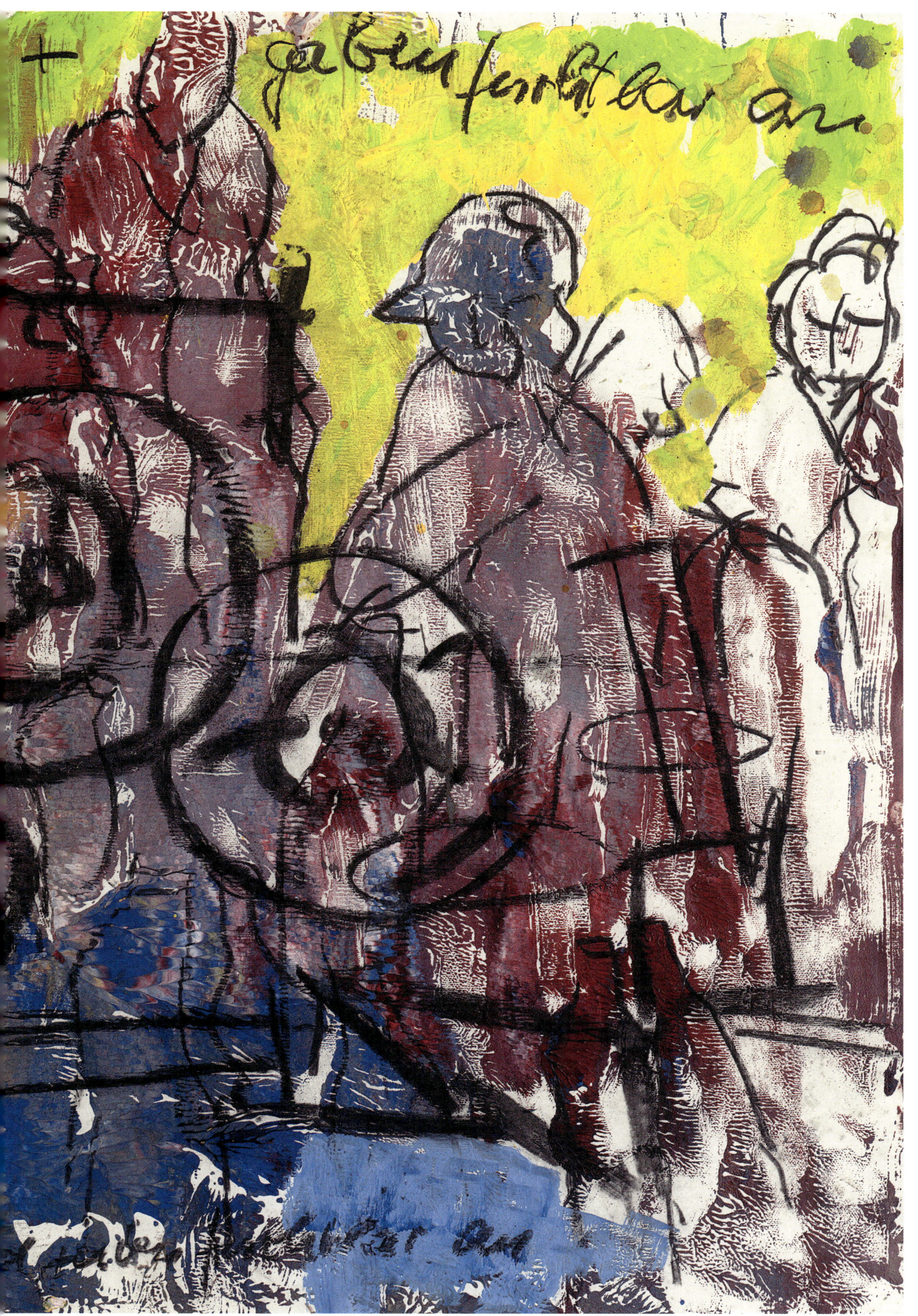

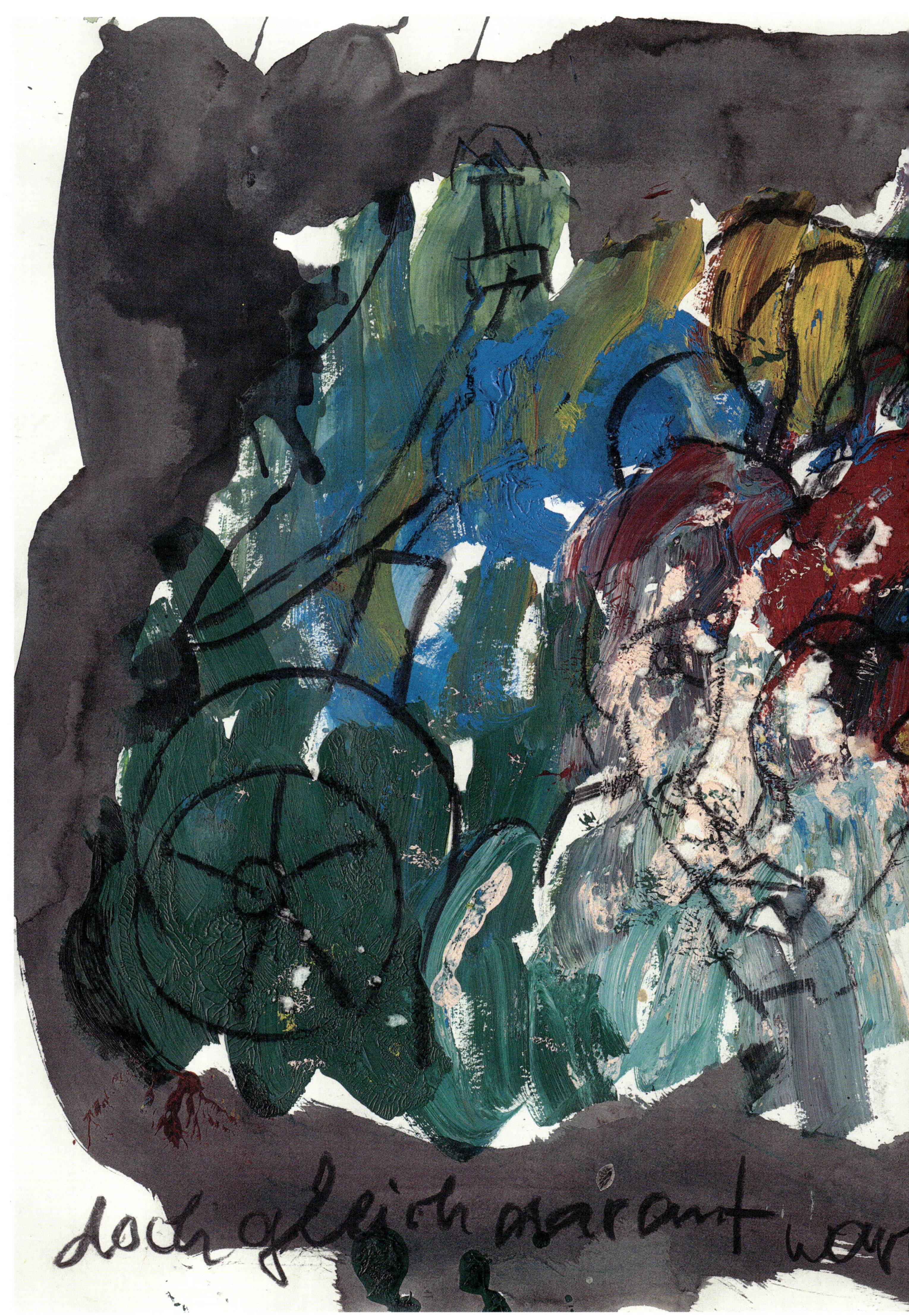

 But shortly afterwards / They confessed—of sins aware

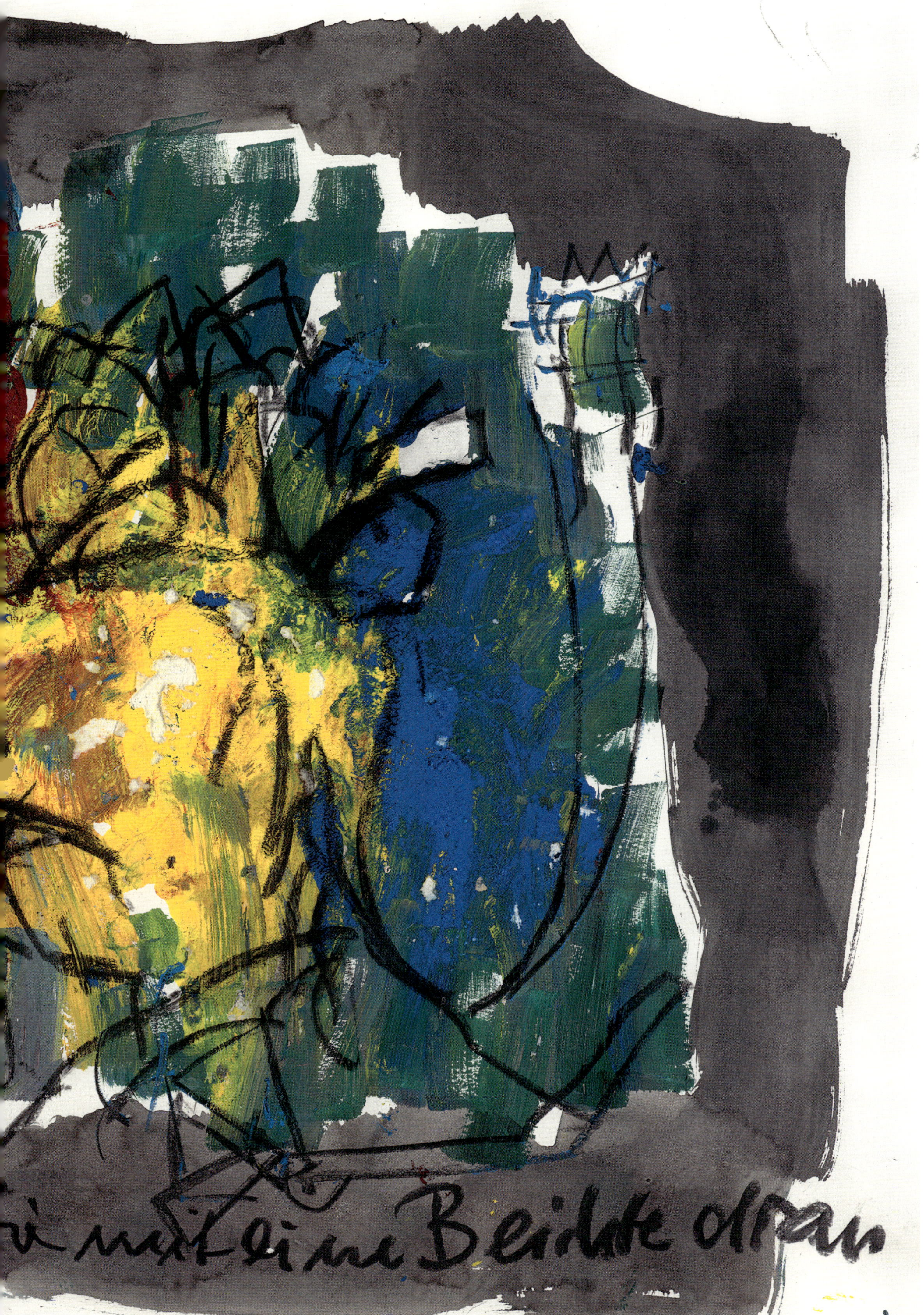
u mit keine Beichte dran

Bragging

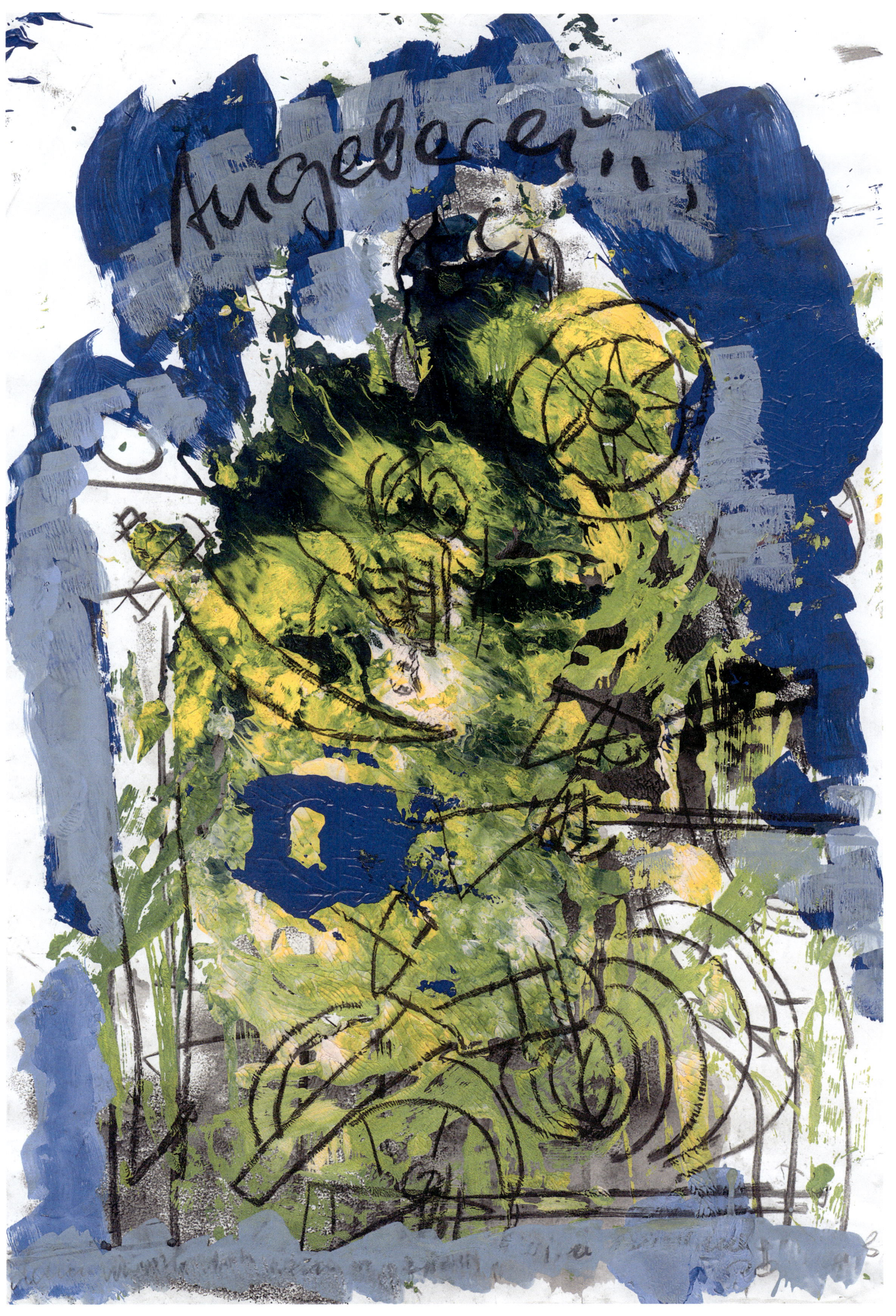

Angeboren

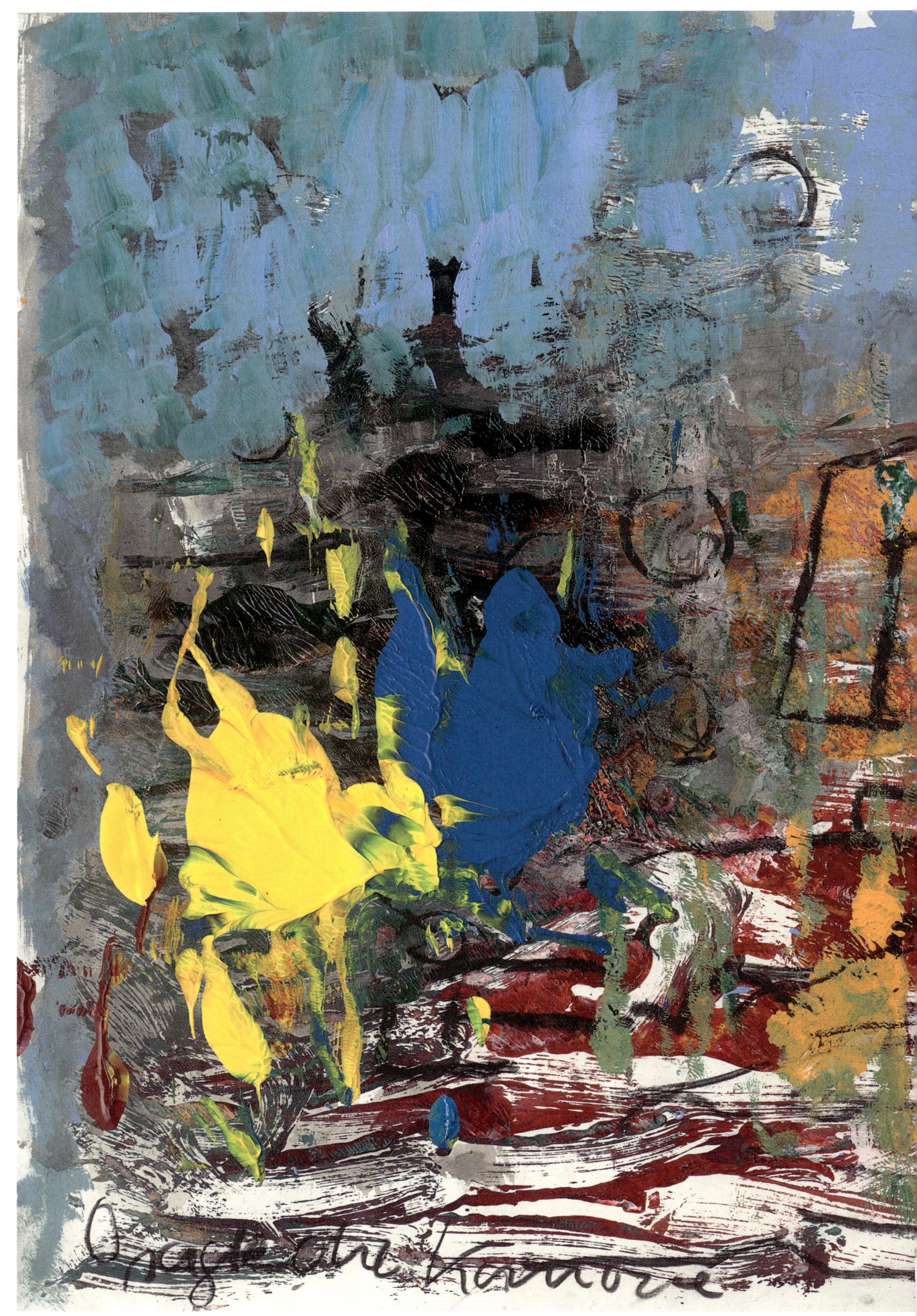

Oh said the cannon proud / I needed only once to boom

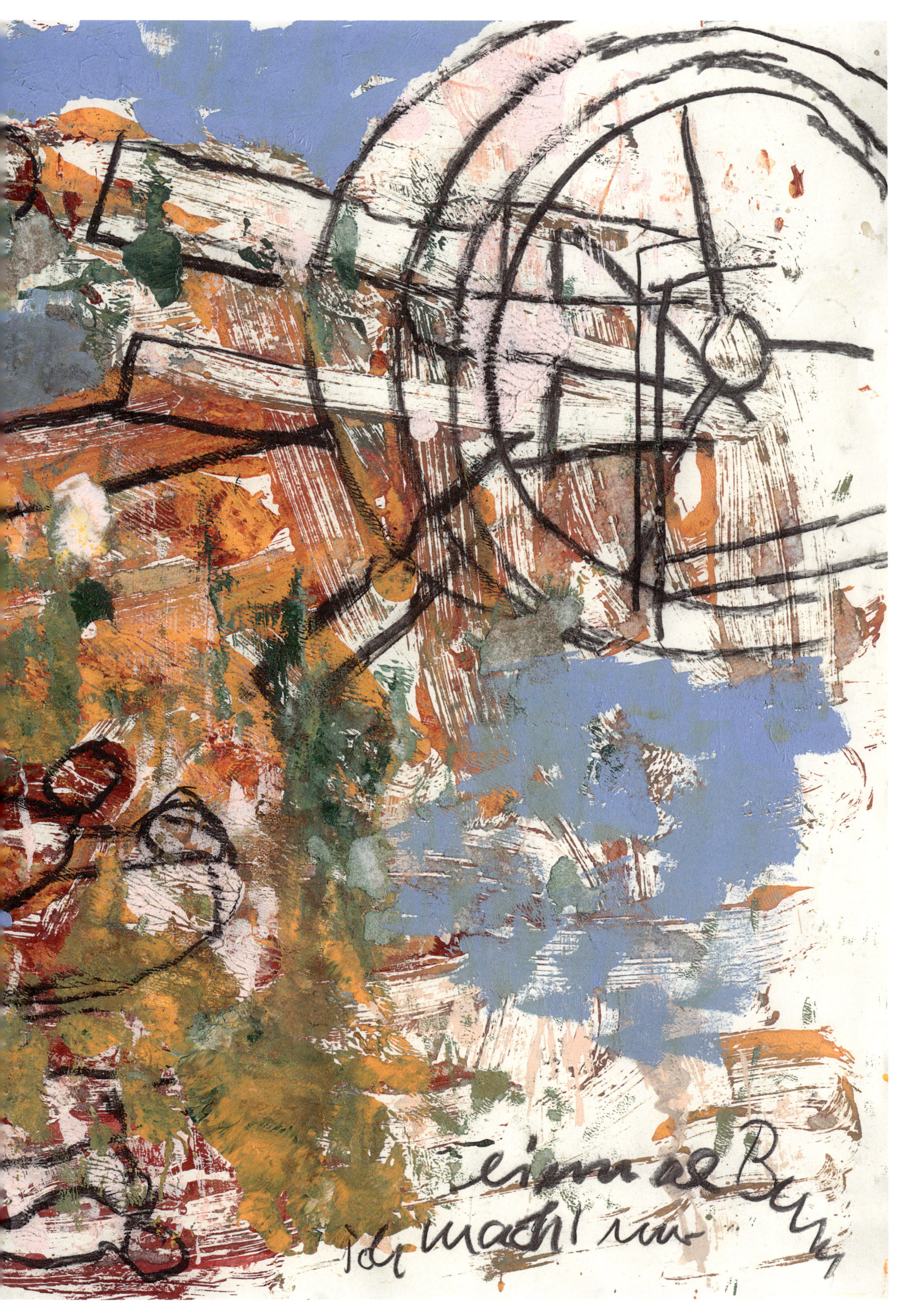

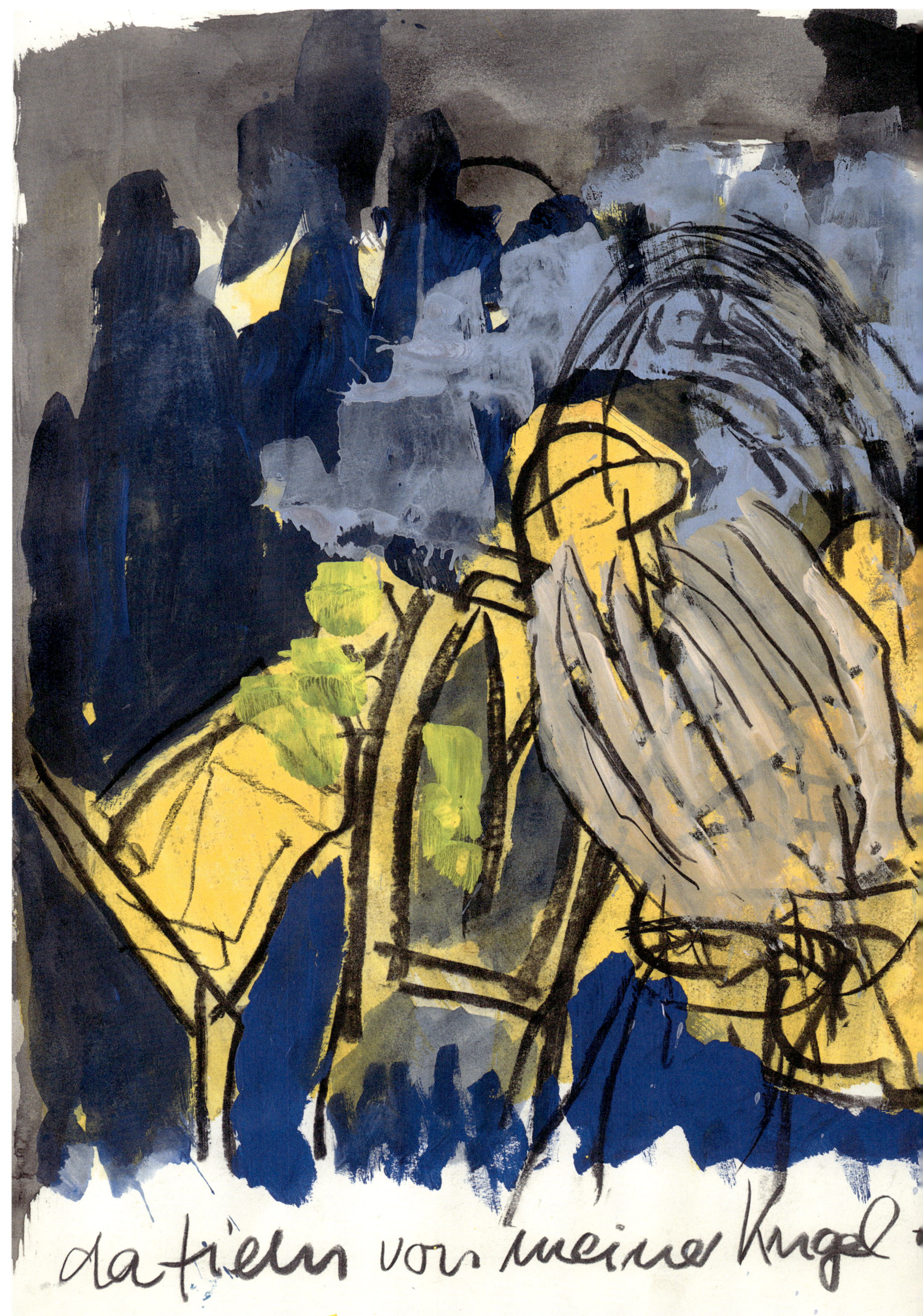

And with only one large cannon ball / Ten regiments met their doom

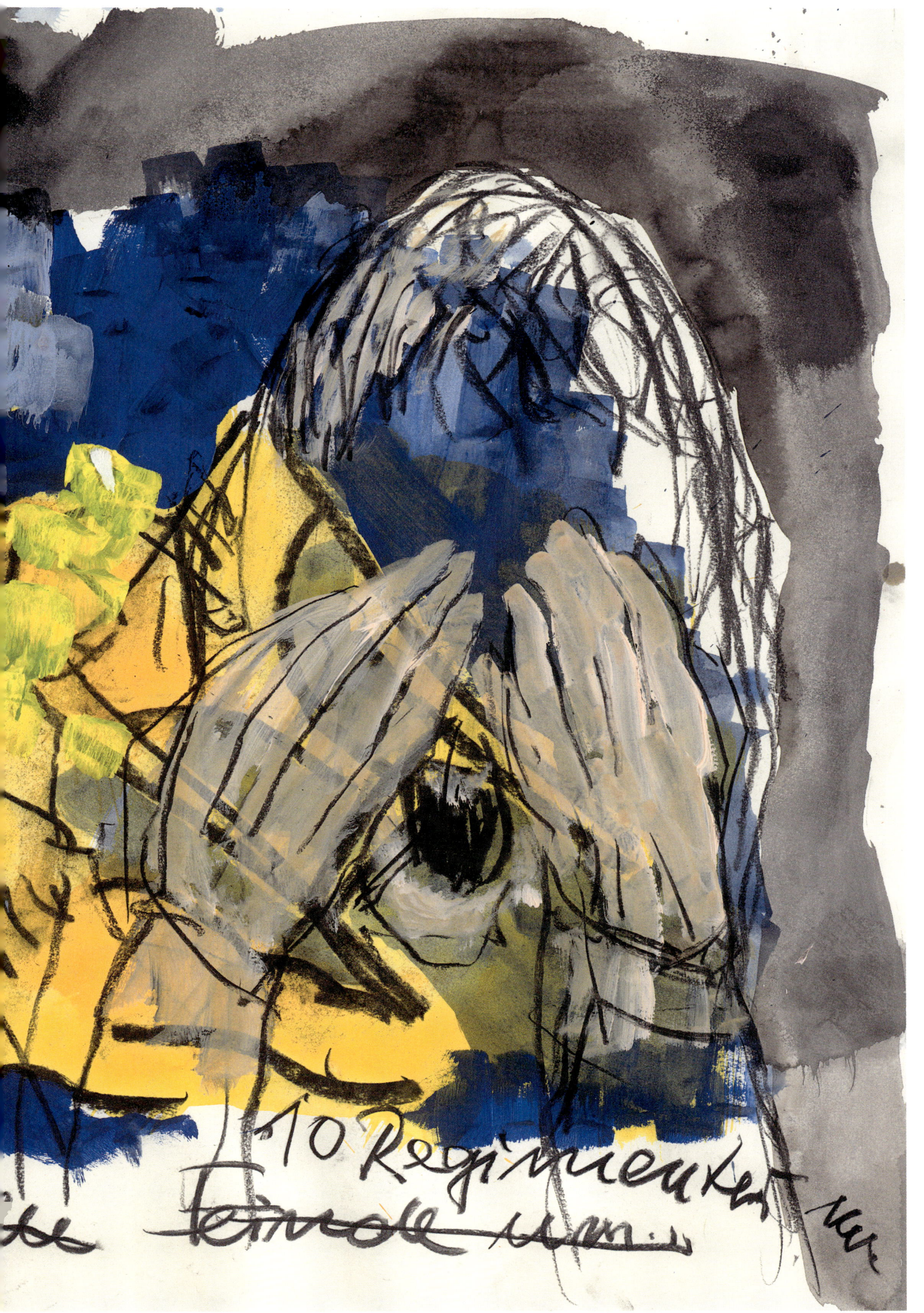

10 Regimenter

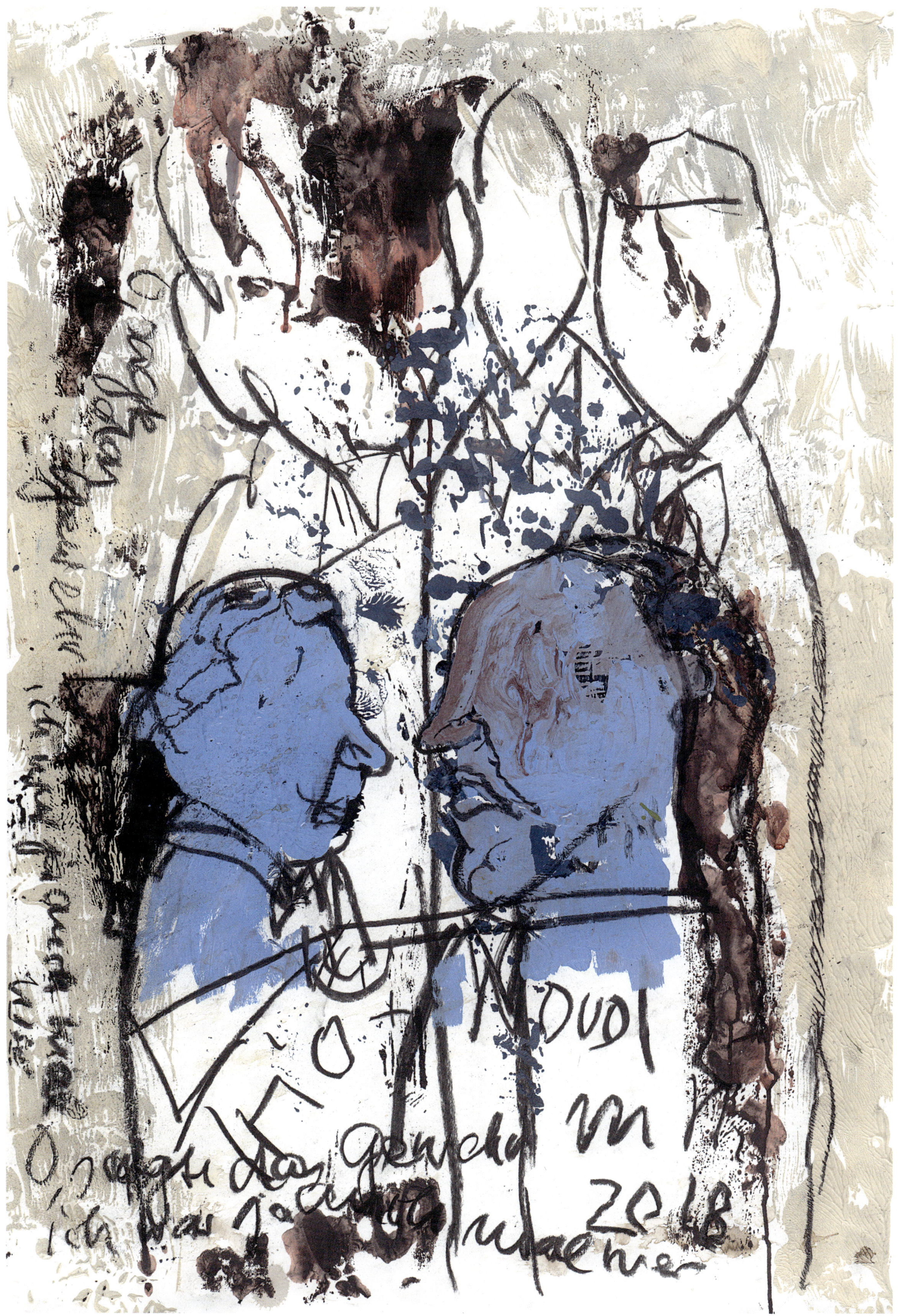

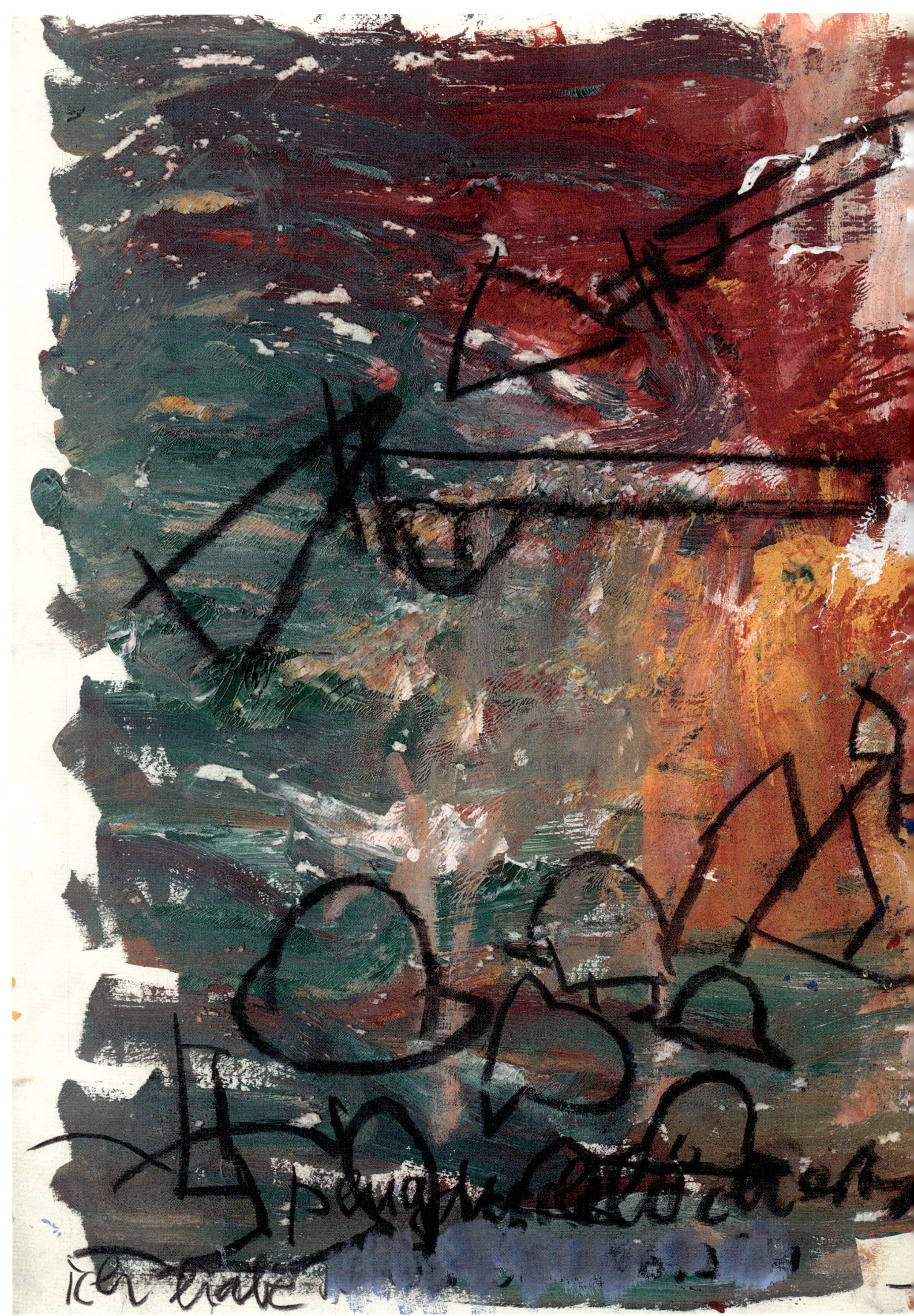

I shot peng full of holes / The city and its troops

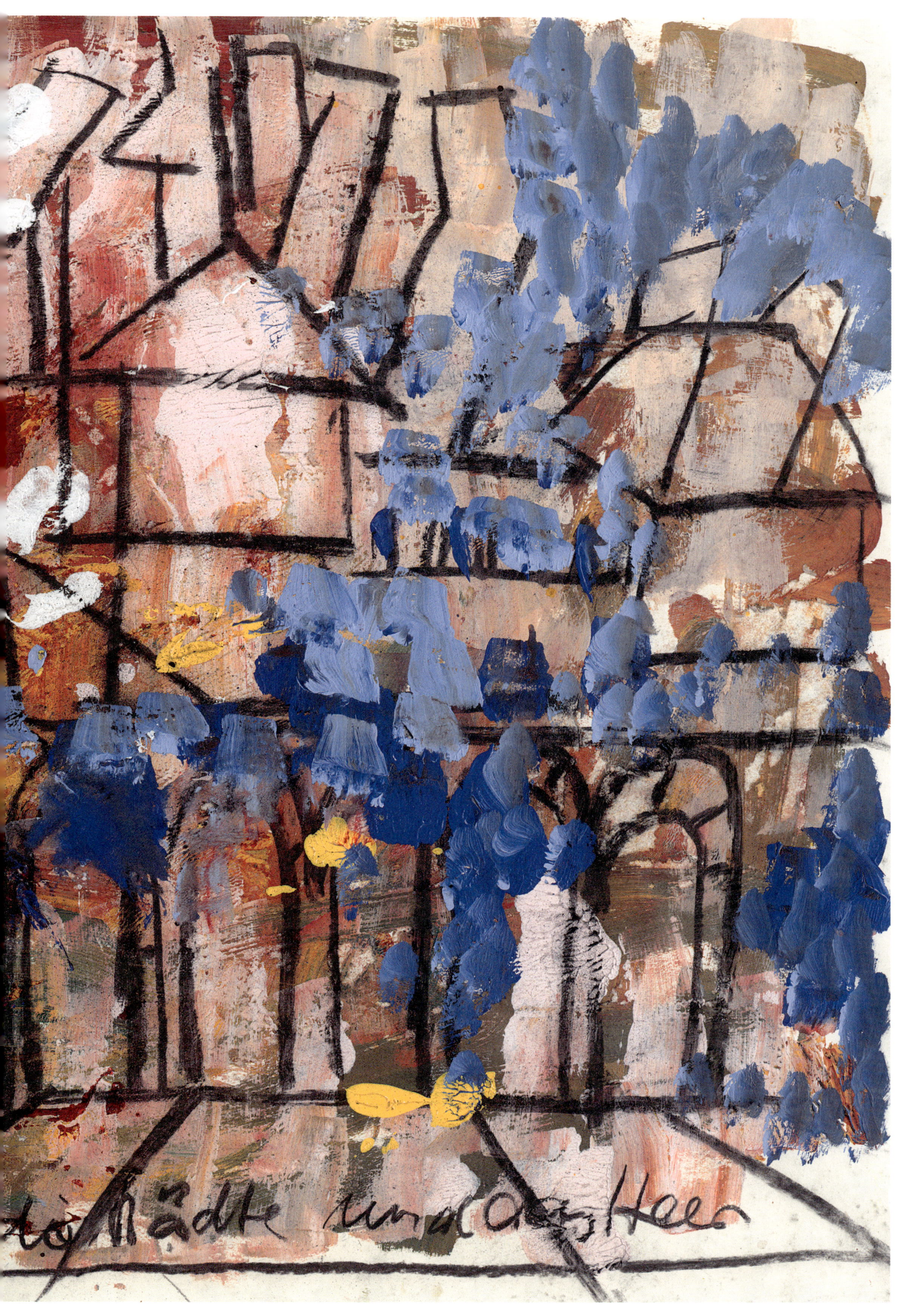

Städte und das Heer

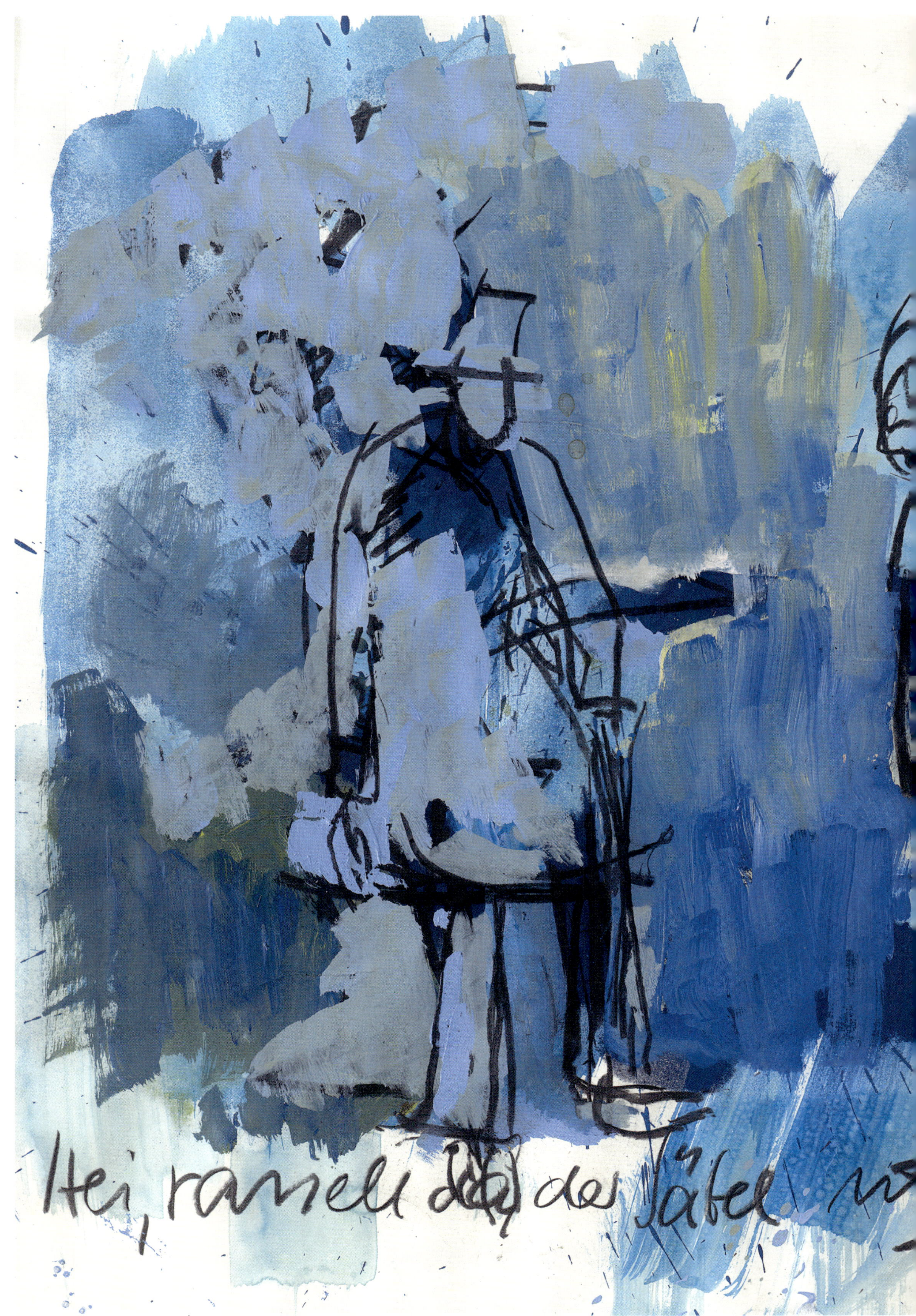

Hey returned the saber / With one fell swoop did I

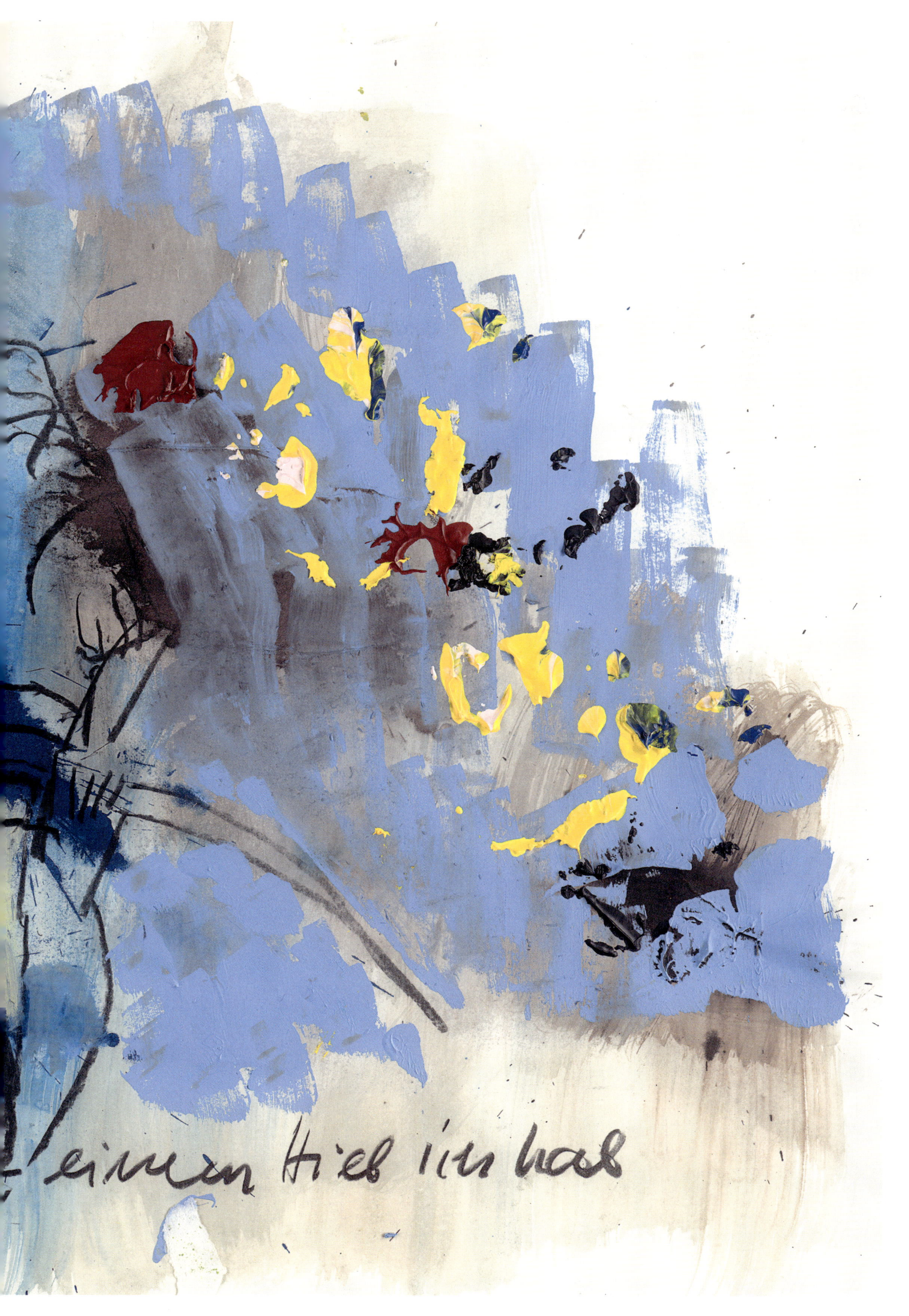
einen Hieb im hals

Mow down the king and with one strike / Several heads did fly

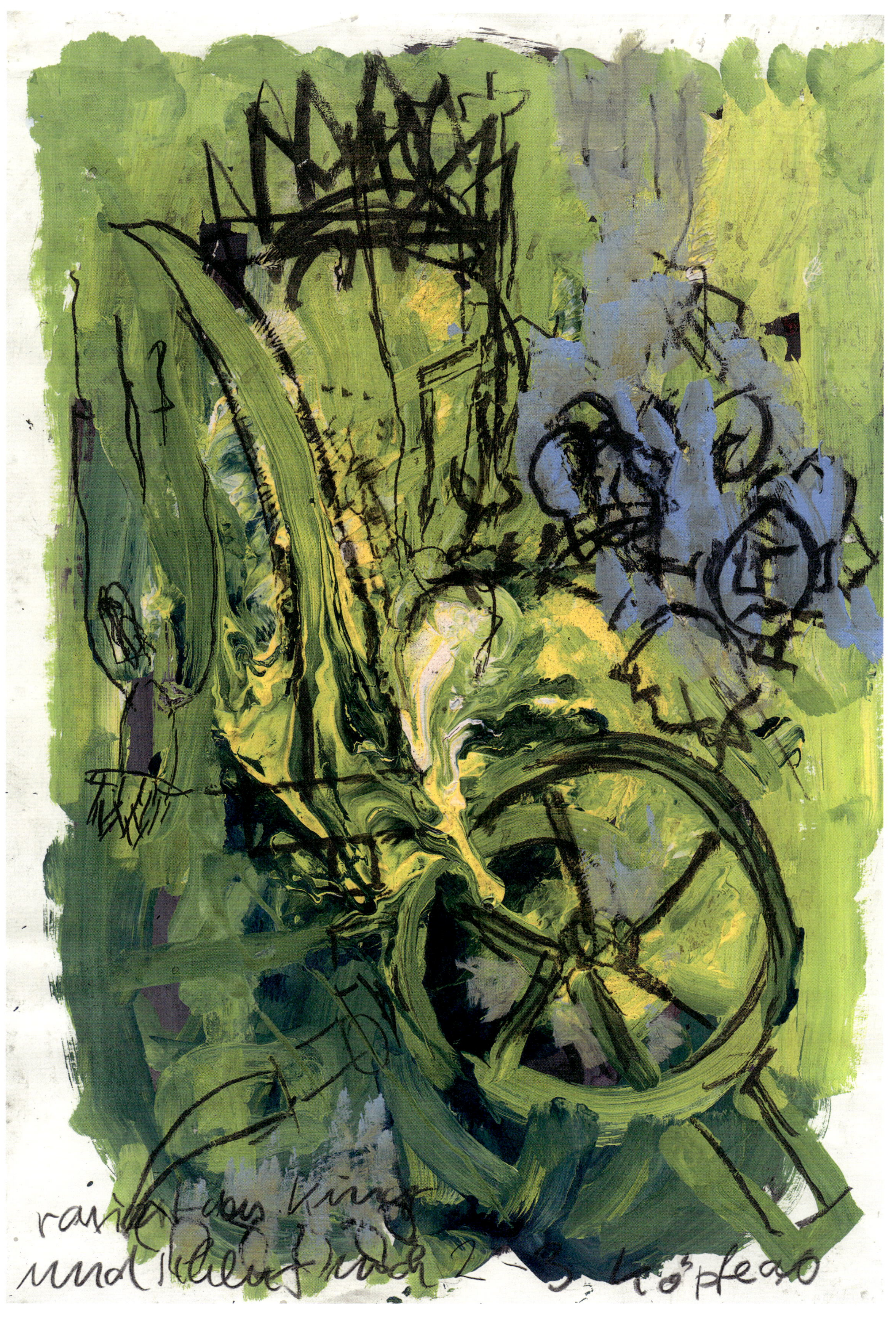
raßt das Ding
und bleibt doch 2–3 Köpfe

Confession

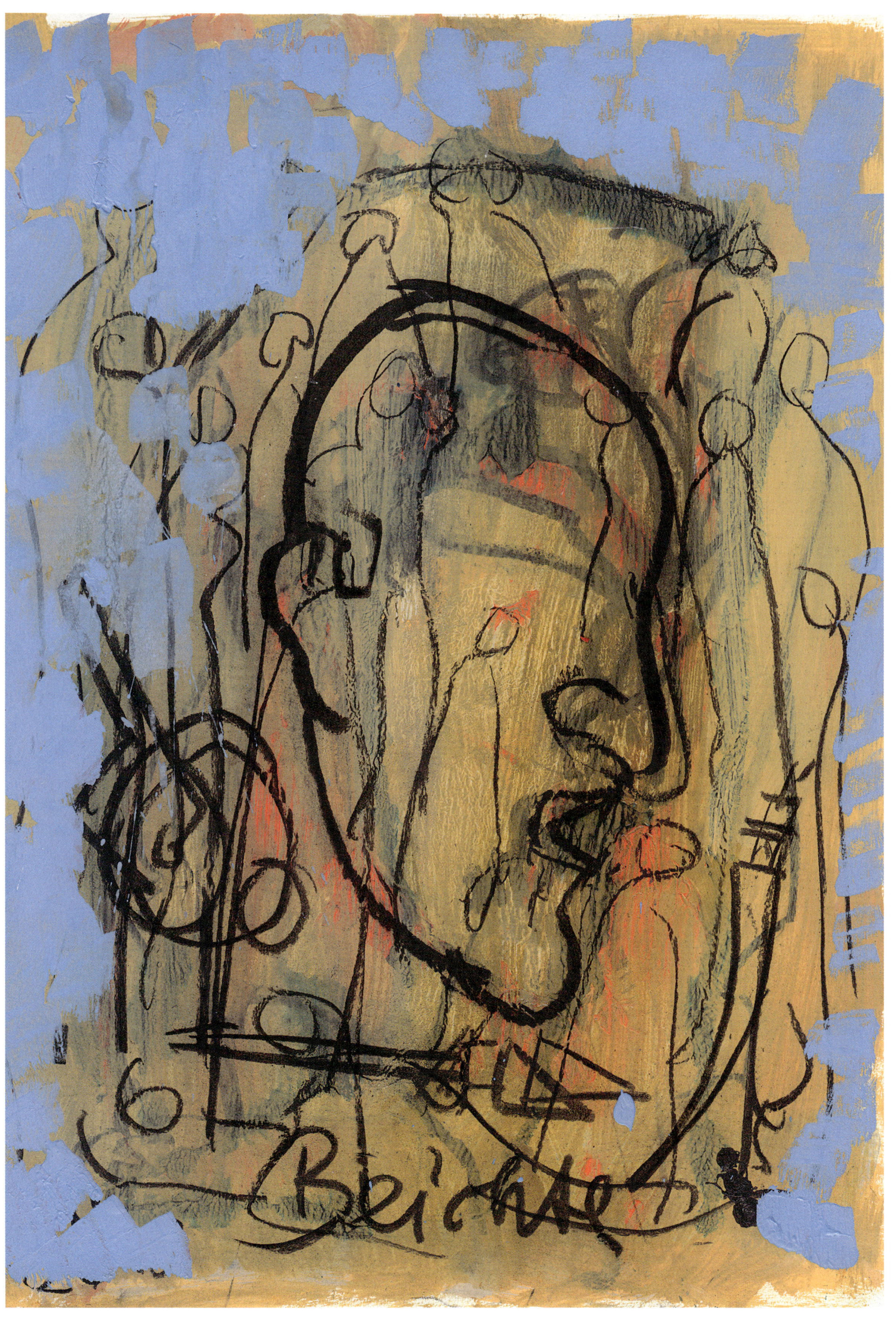
Beichte

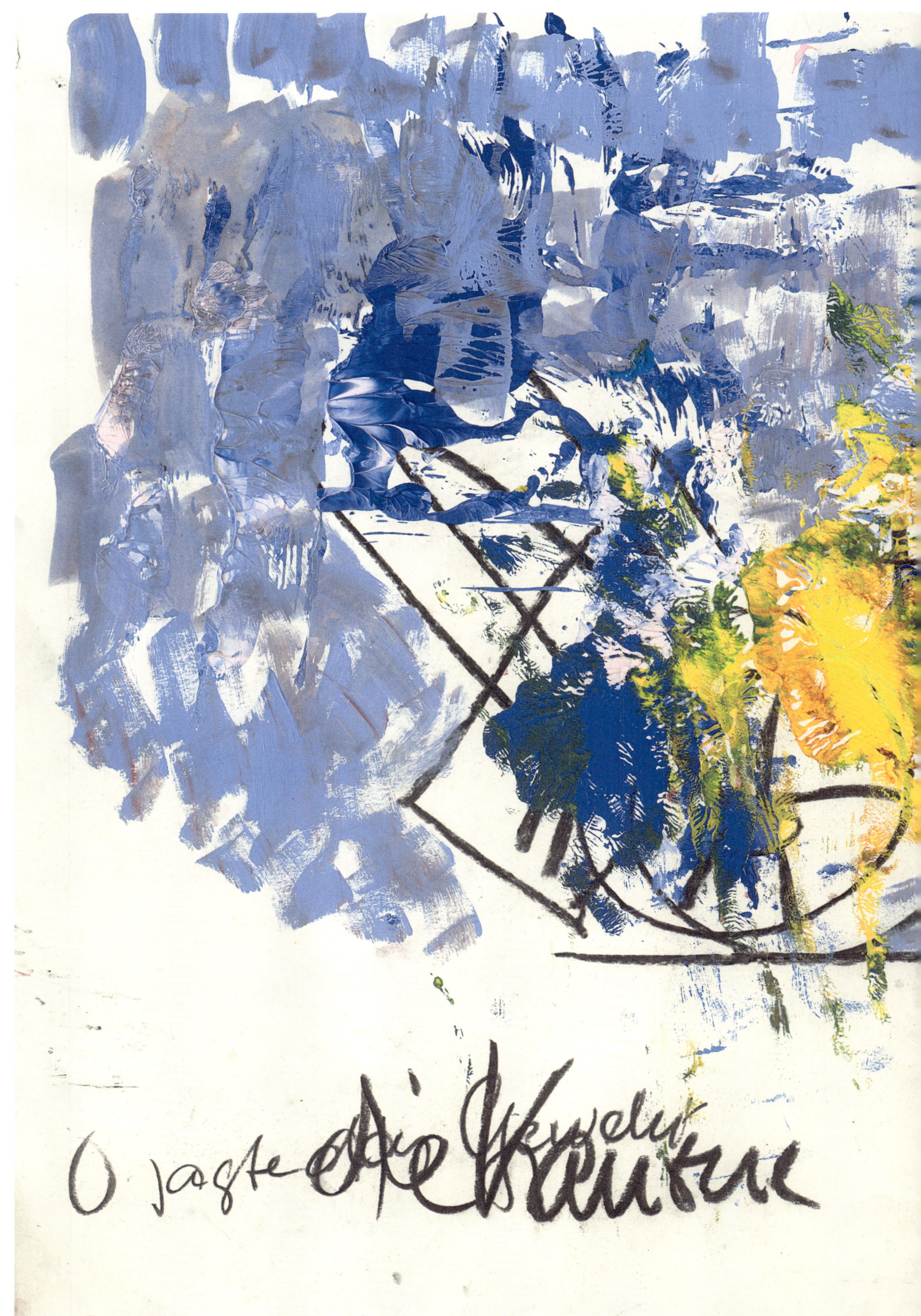

O said the cannon proud / I wish I were a train

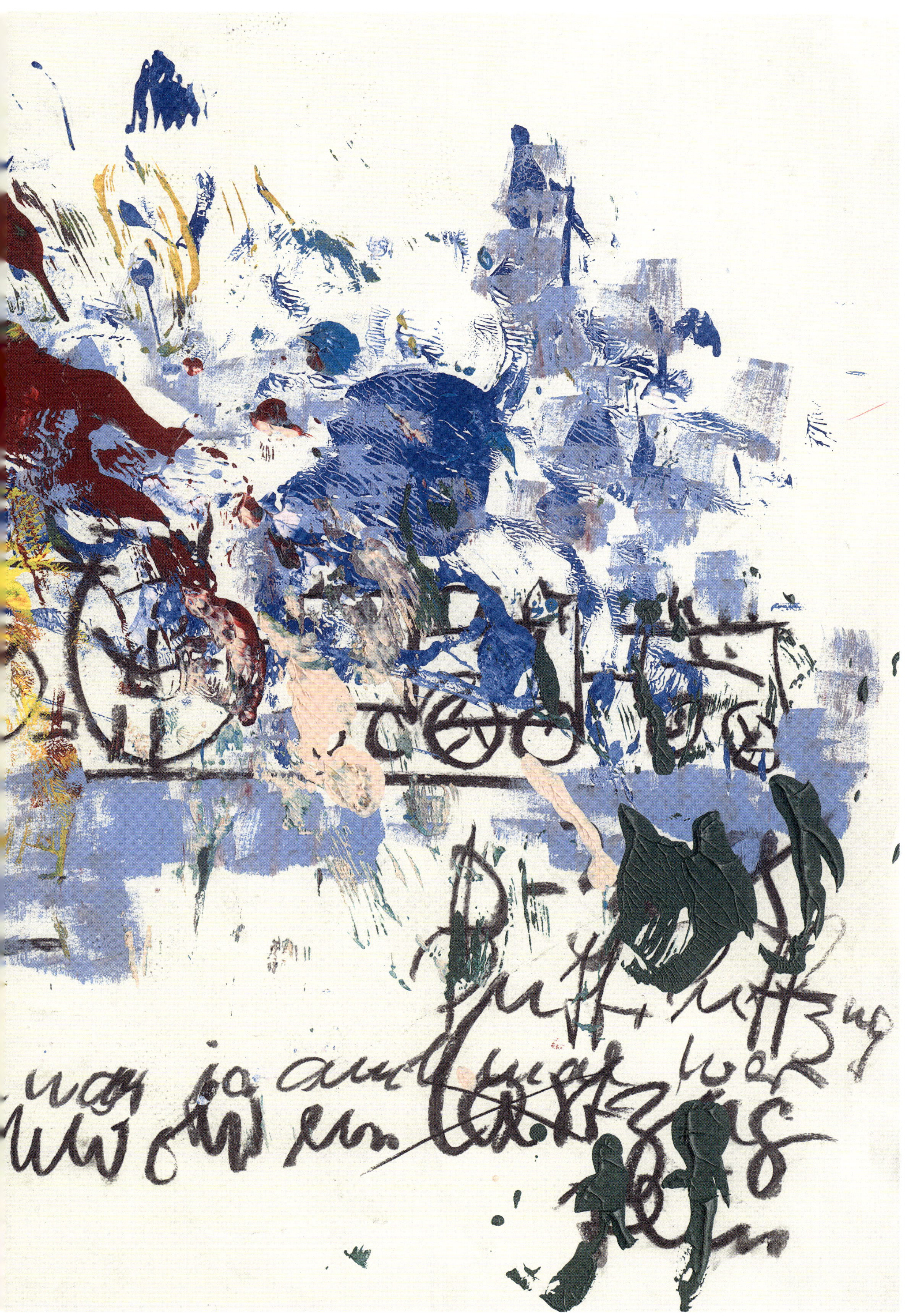

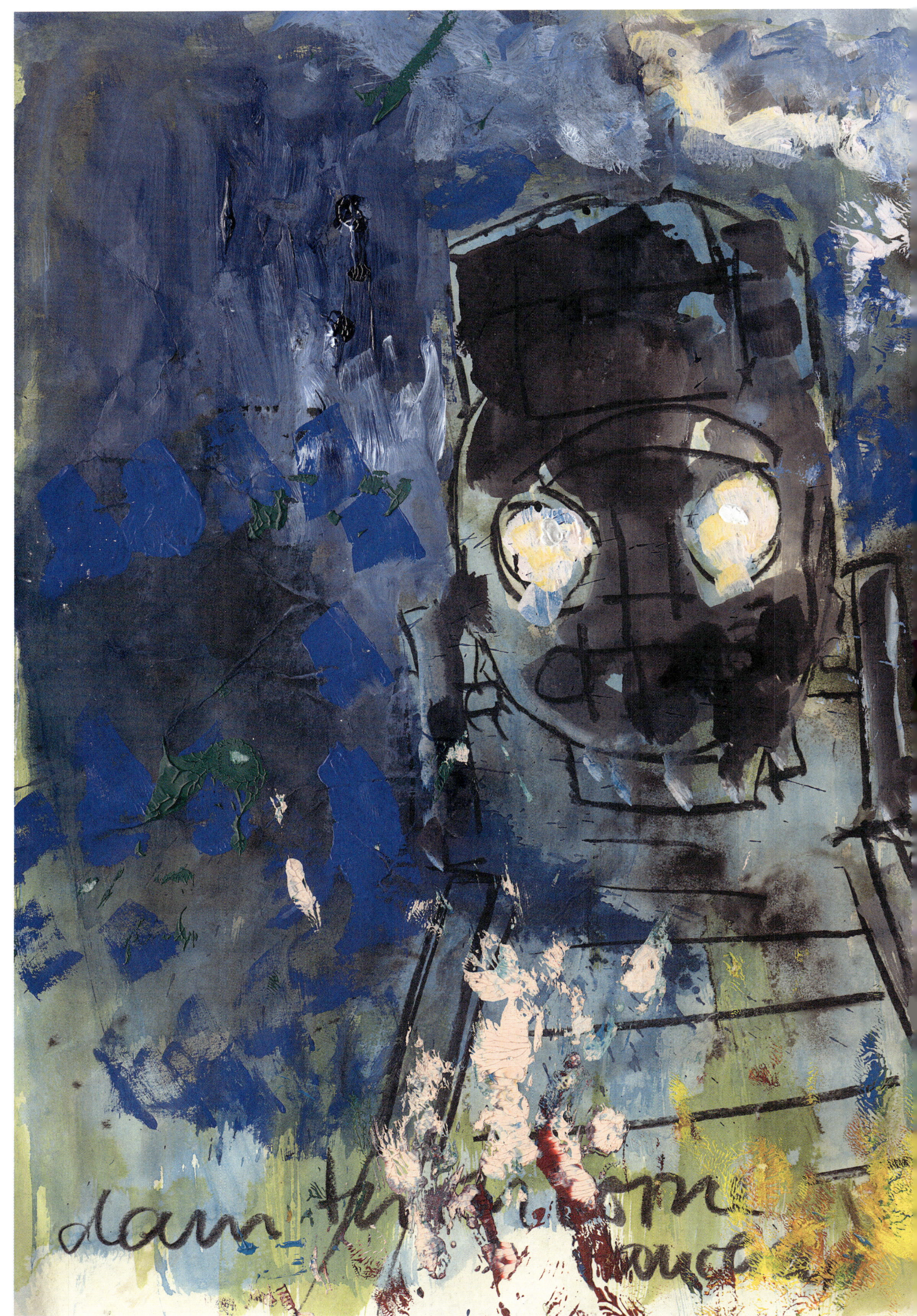

Then I would smoke away up front / And halt my shooting brain

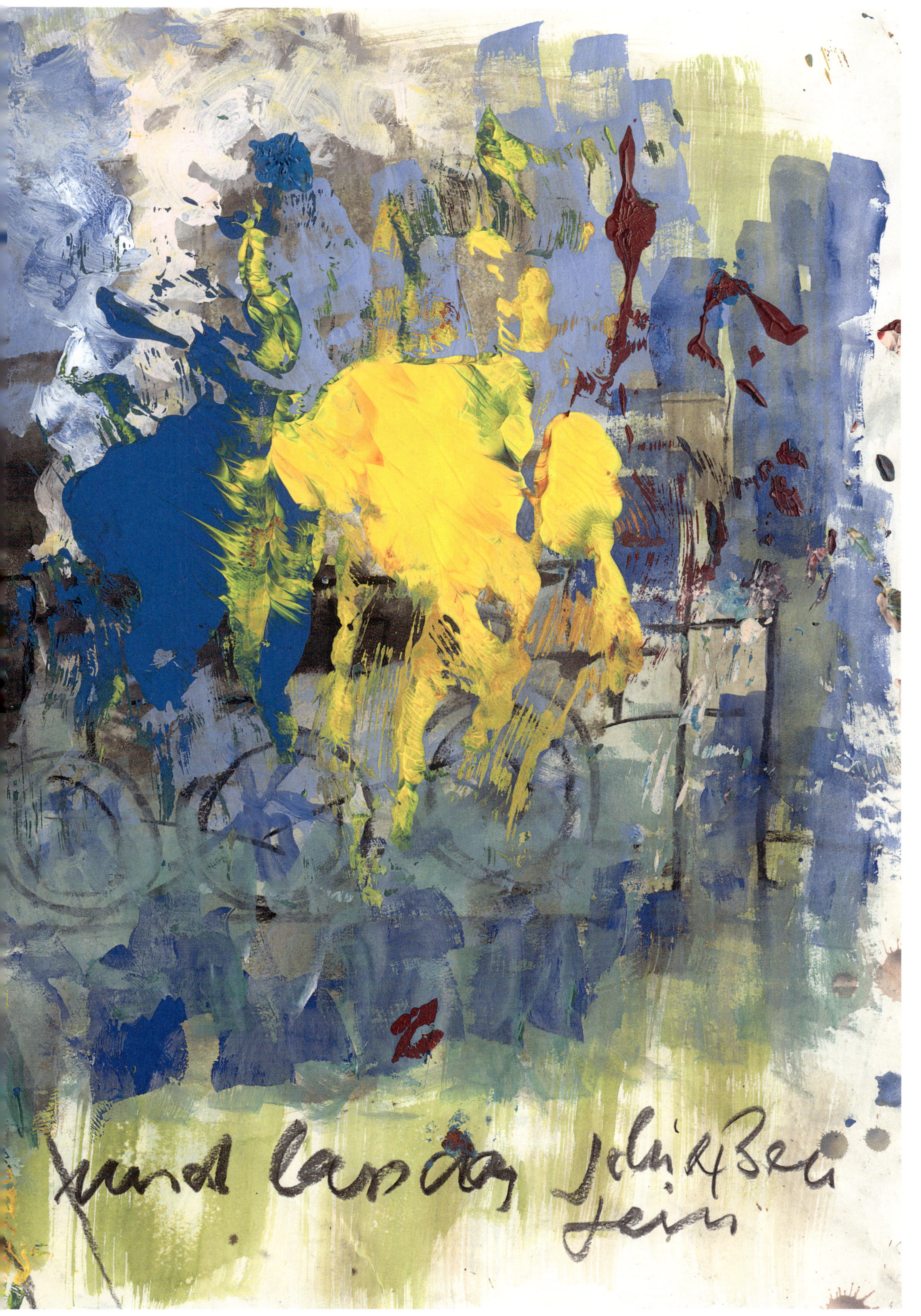

Or an auto I would like to be / Said the rifle then I'd know

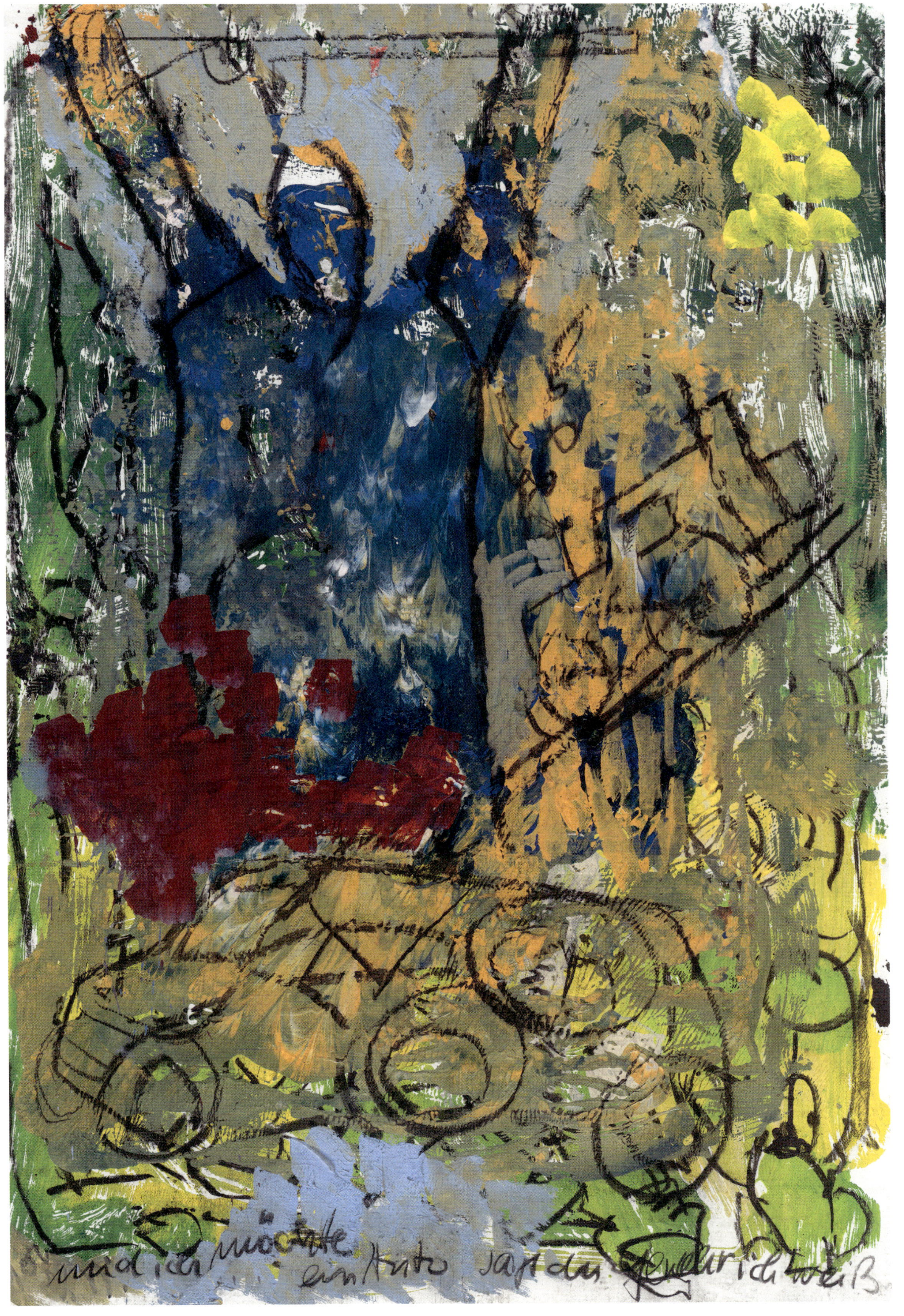
und ich möchte ein Auto sagt du weil ich weiß

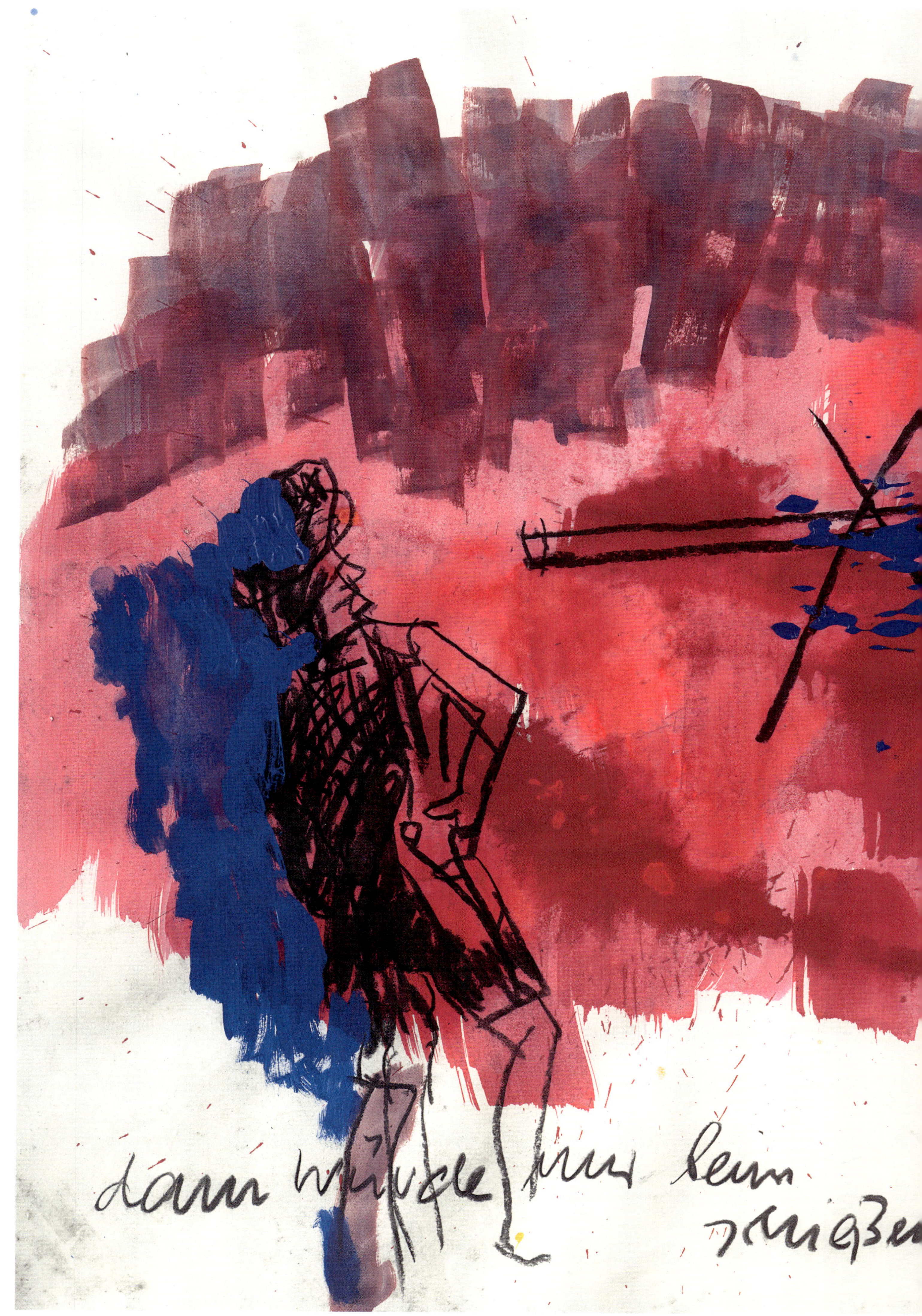

That when I'd be a' shooting / My neck wouldn't hurt me so

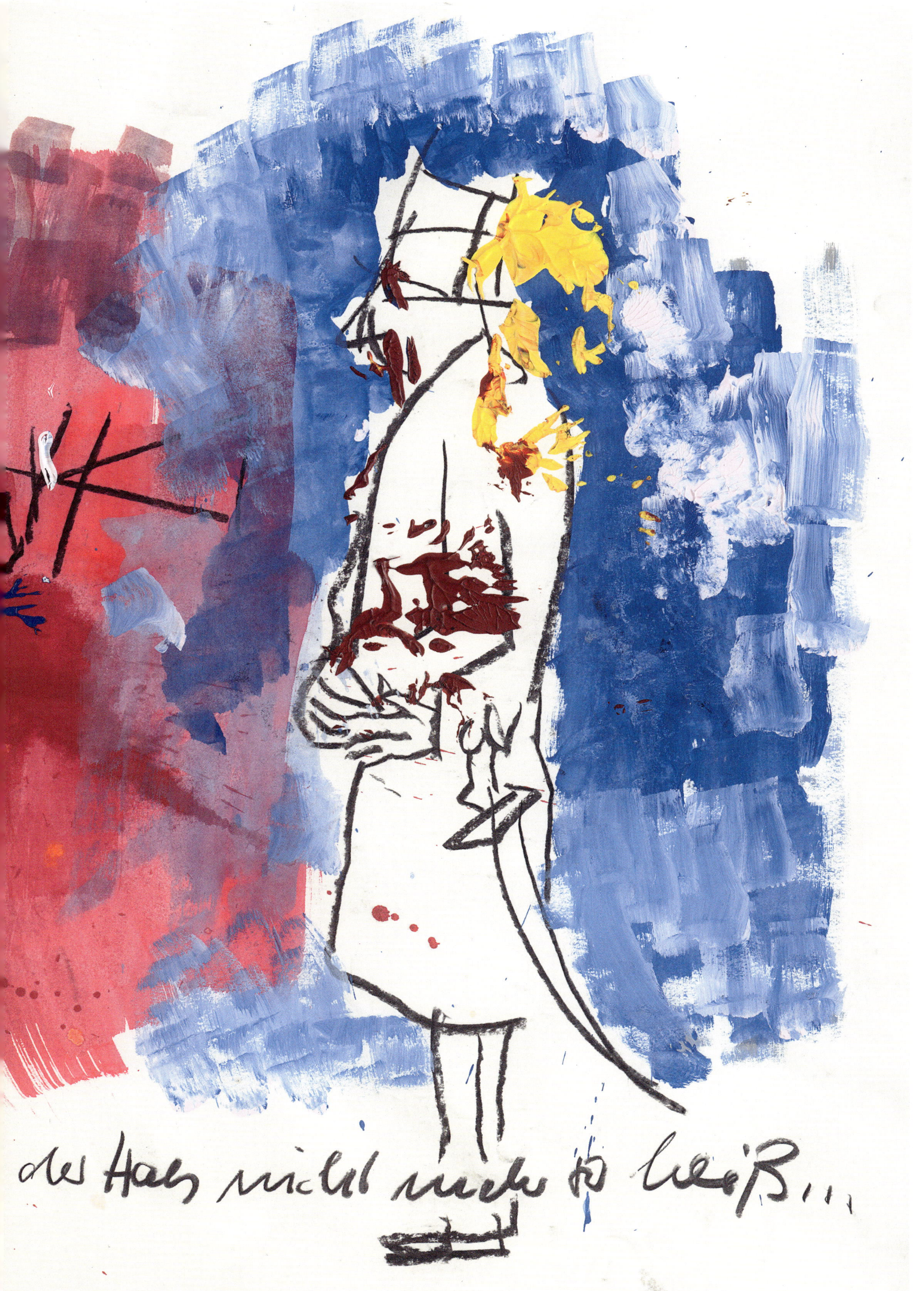
des Hals nicht mehr so weiß...

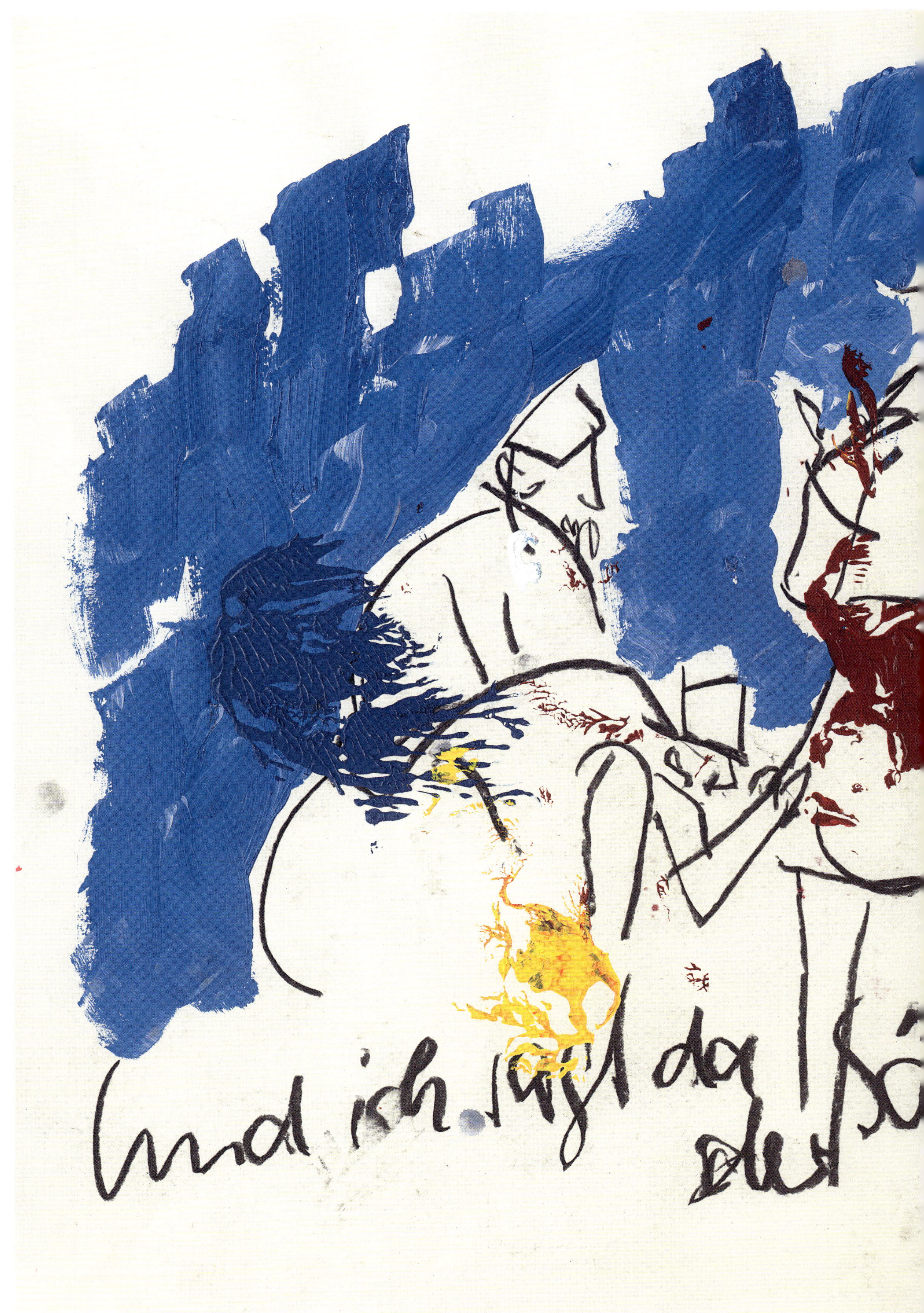

And I said the saber / I'd like to be a knife

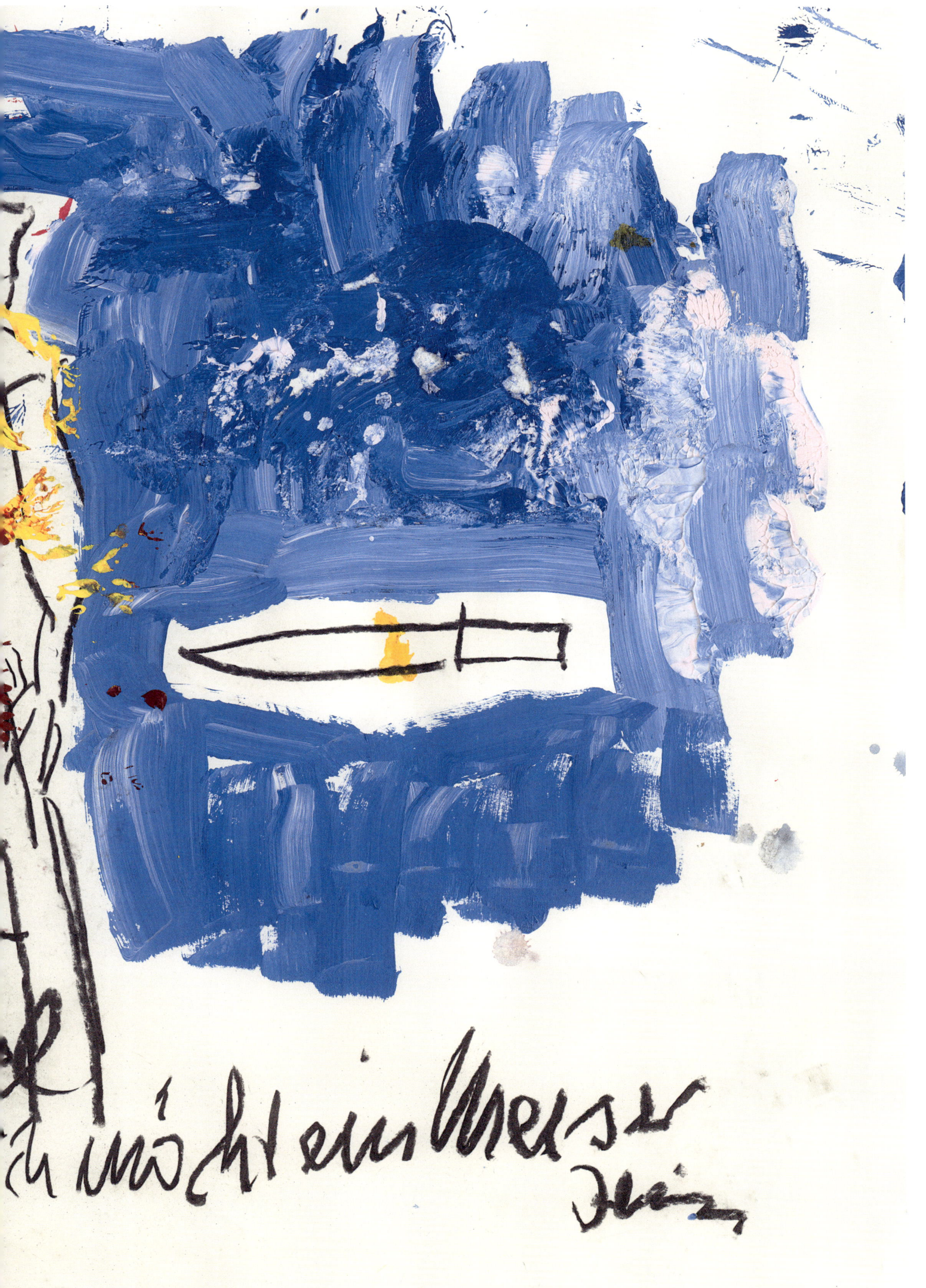
ich möchte ein Messer

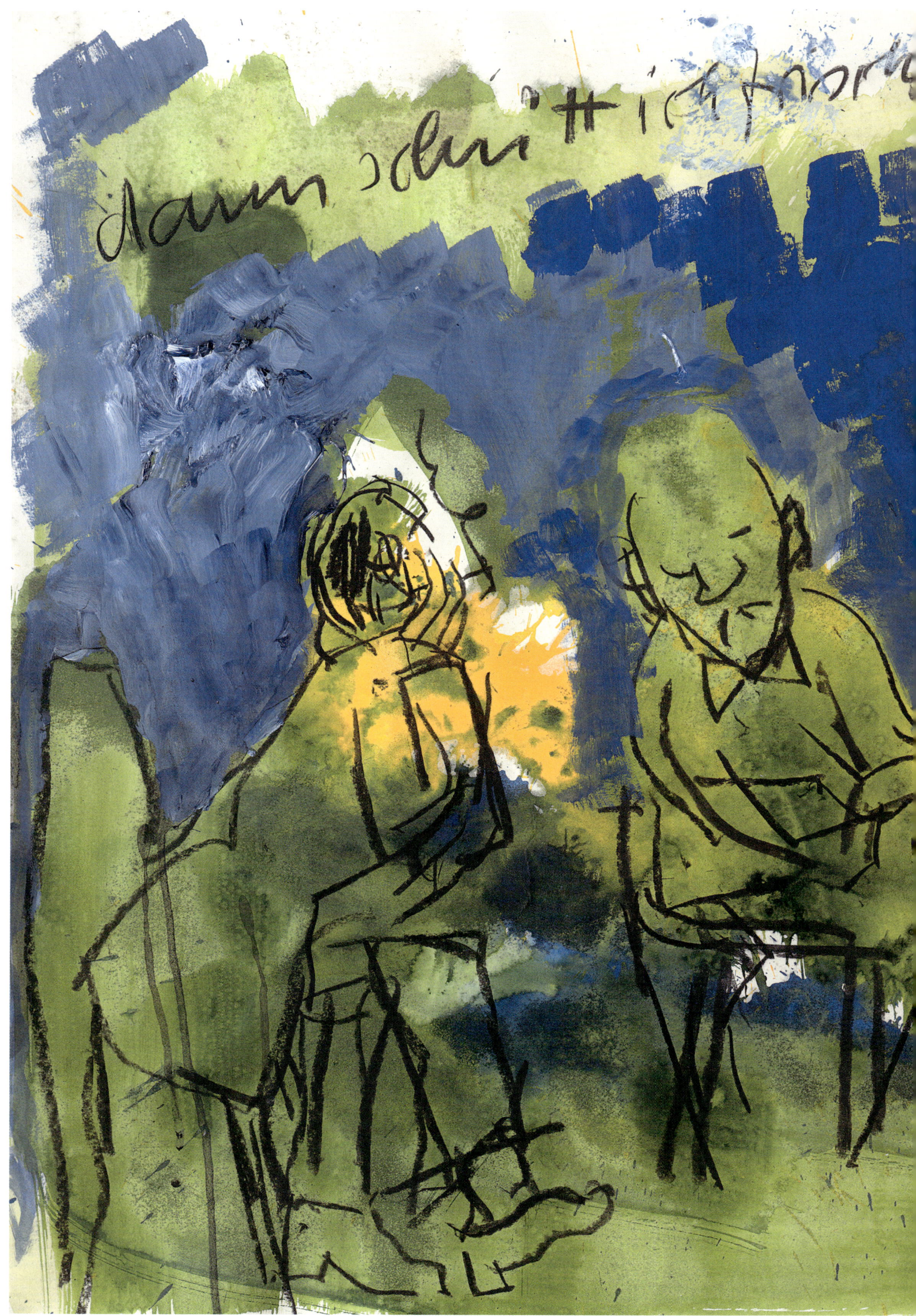

I'd cut some ham and bread and apples / And be happy with my life

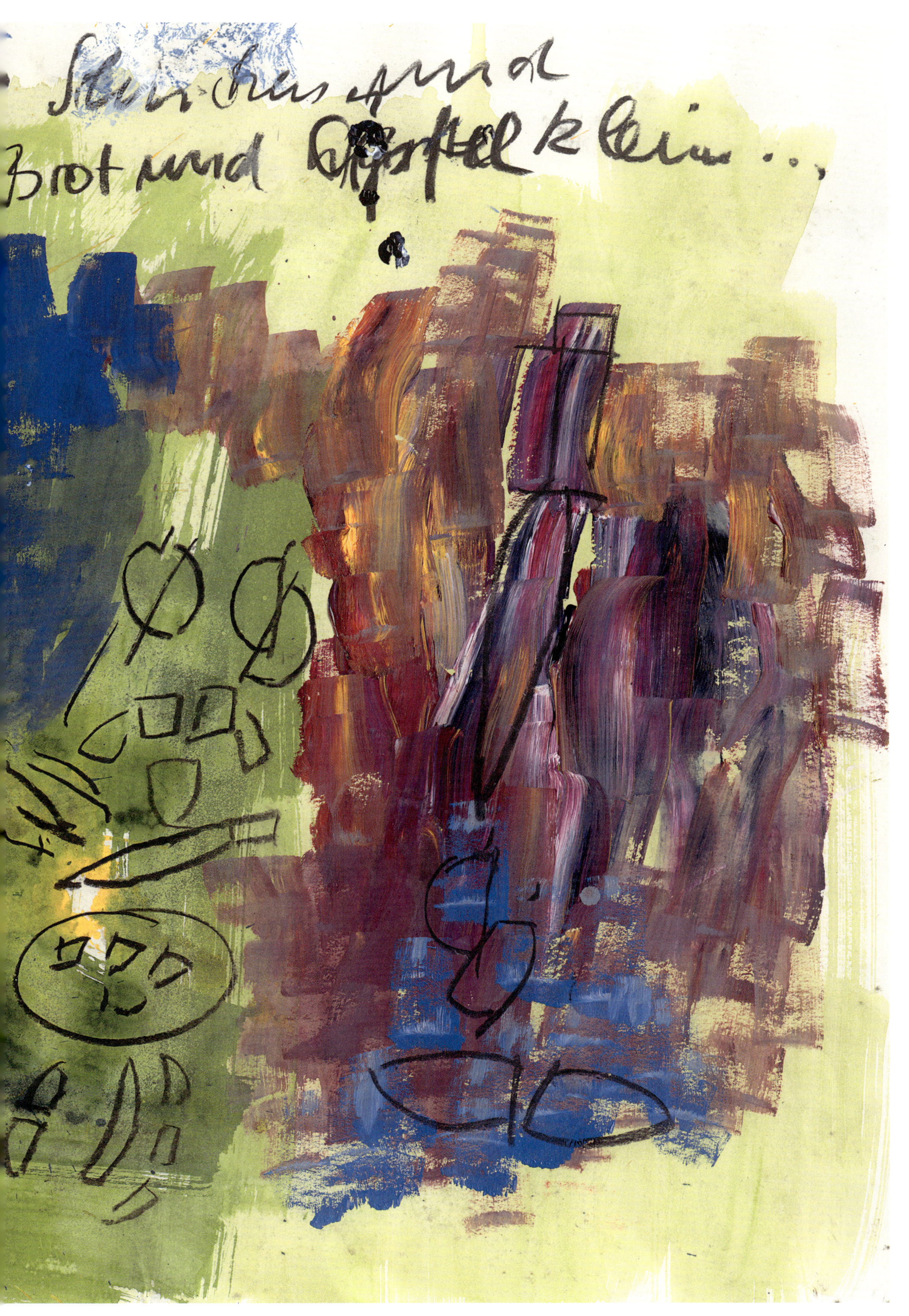
Steirisches und
Brot und Äpfel klein ...

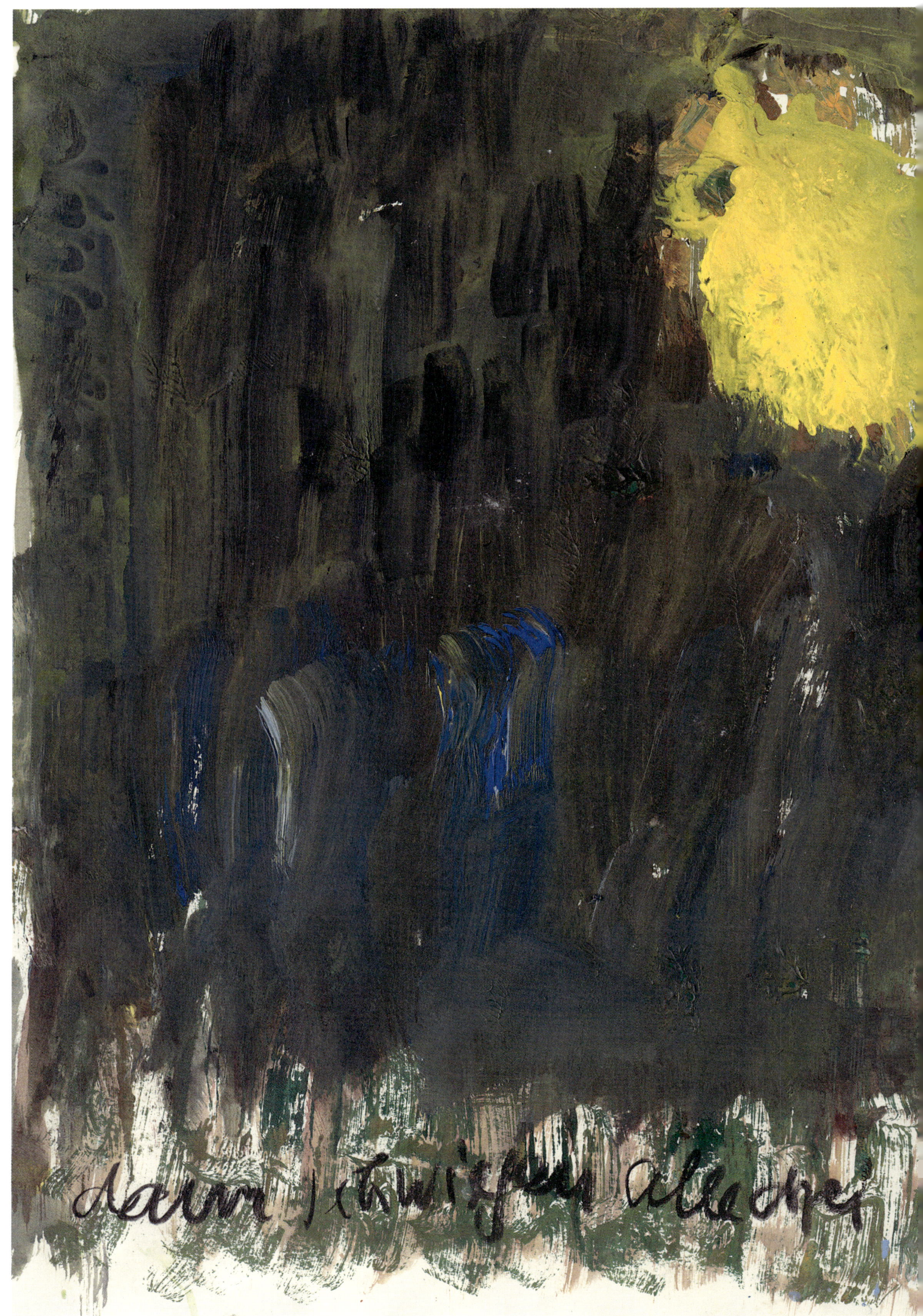

 Then all the three fell silent / In the mild evening light

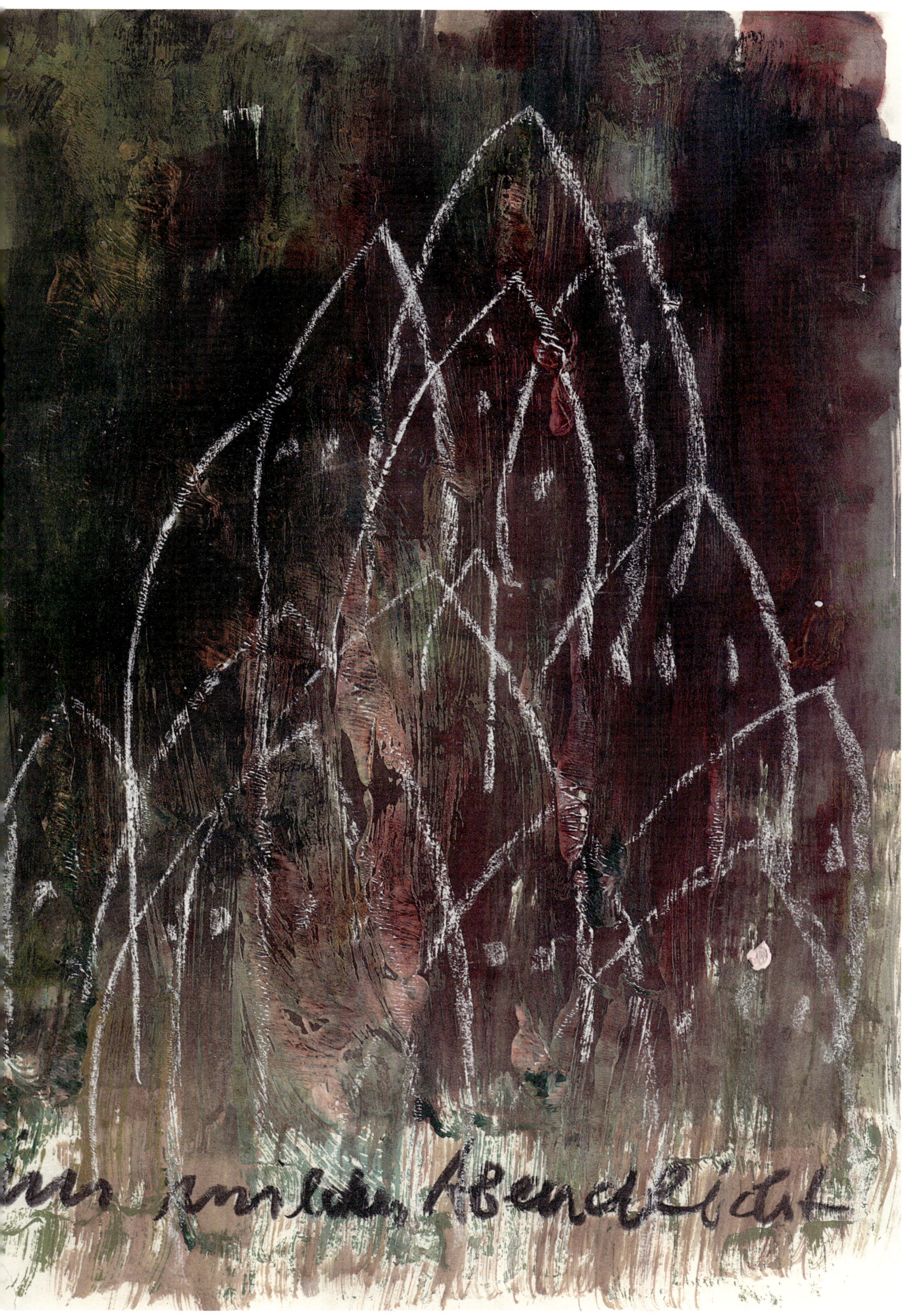
im milden Abendlicht

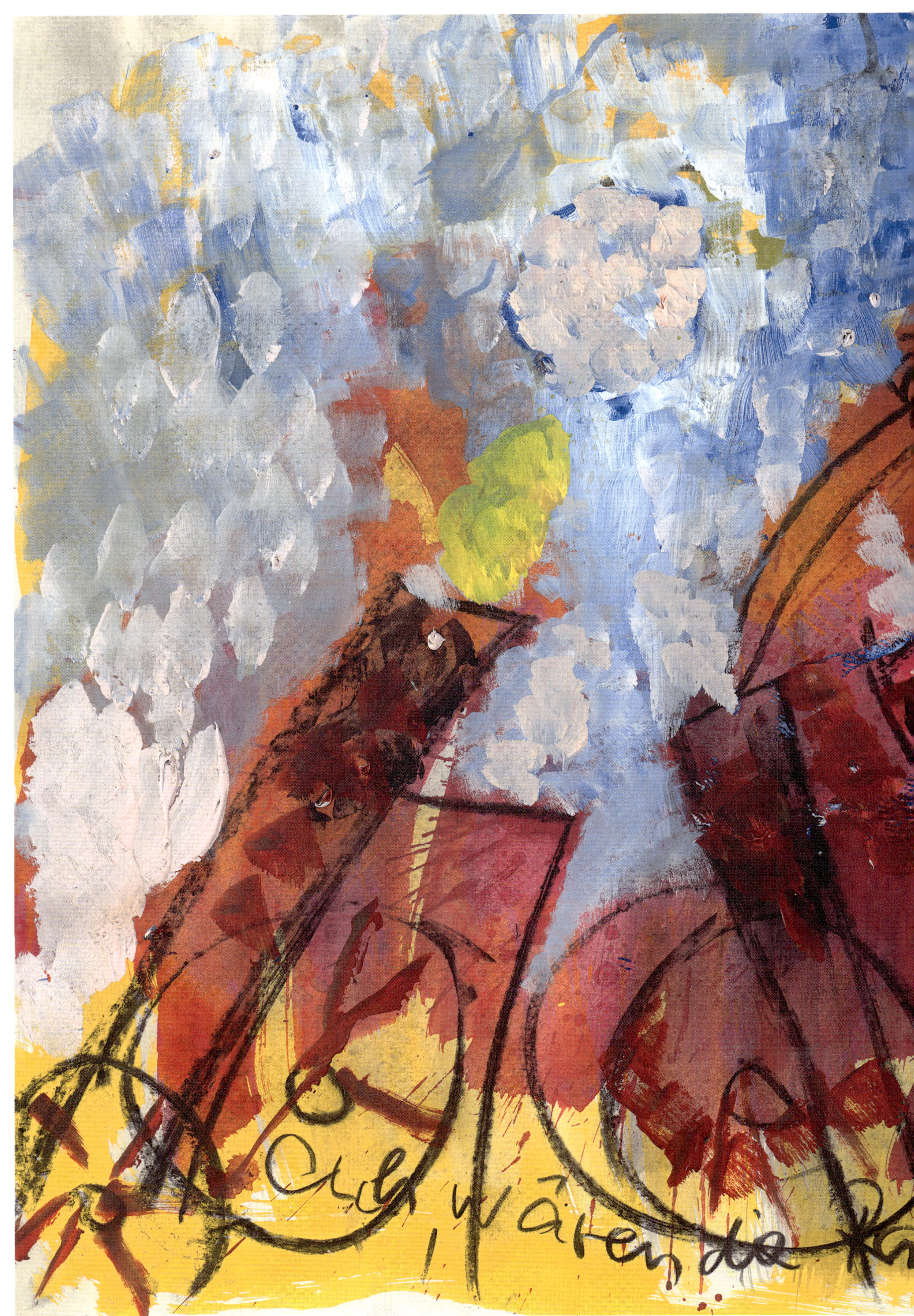

If only the rockets there / Had been shot at the moon so bright

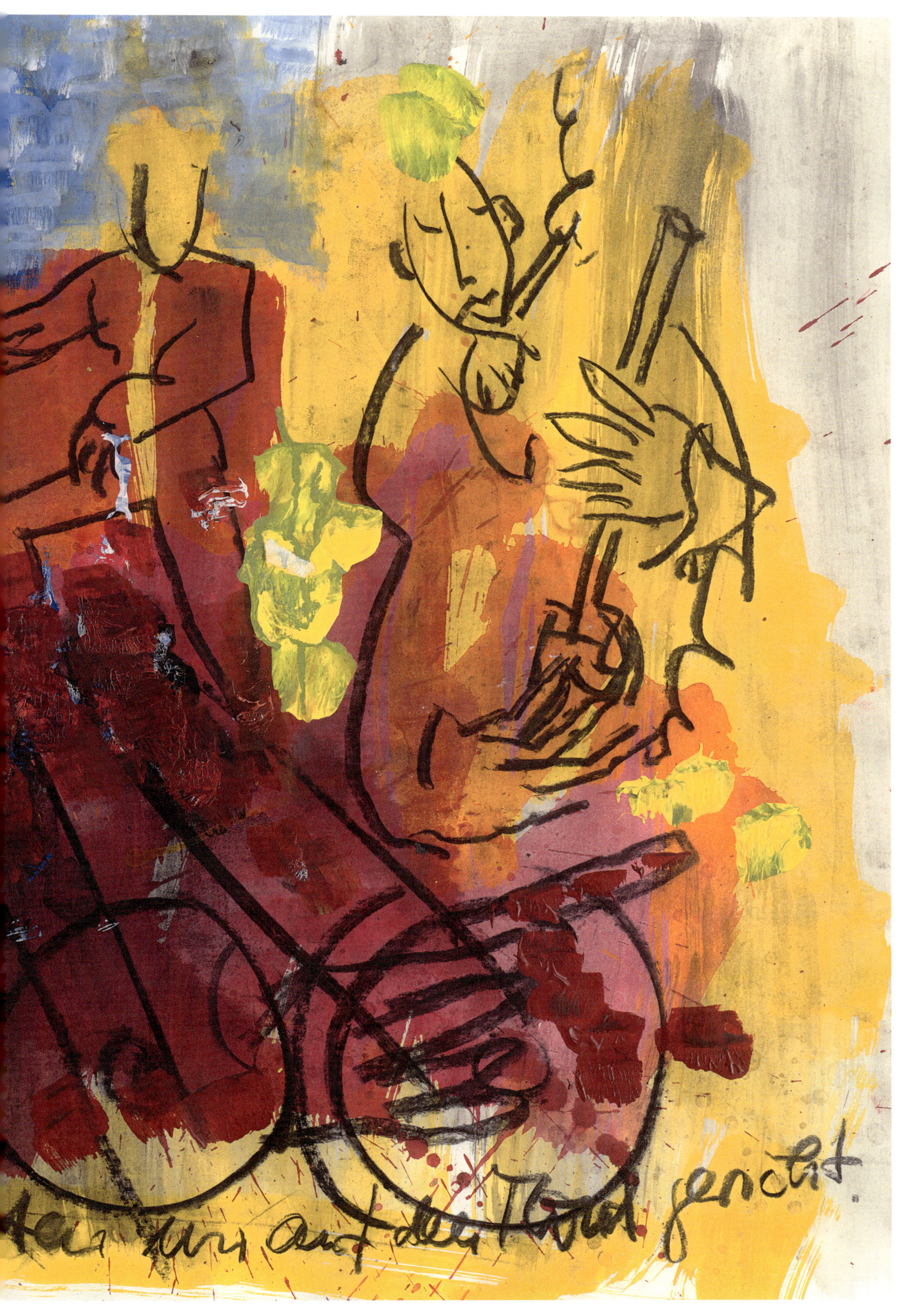

uns auf den Tod gericht.

Nachtrag

Und der Mond?
Raketen auf m...
Nie...
→ Ihr seht mich nicht
→ Ihr trefft mich ni...
→ ...bin kein T... raus
...ich bin
Ich schalt das Mond...
einfach aus
und dann?
Nix... Schwarz... ke...
kein Mo...

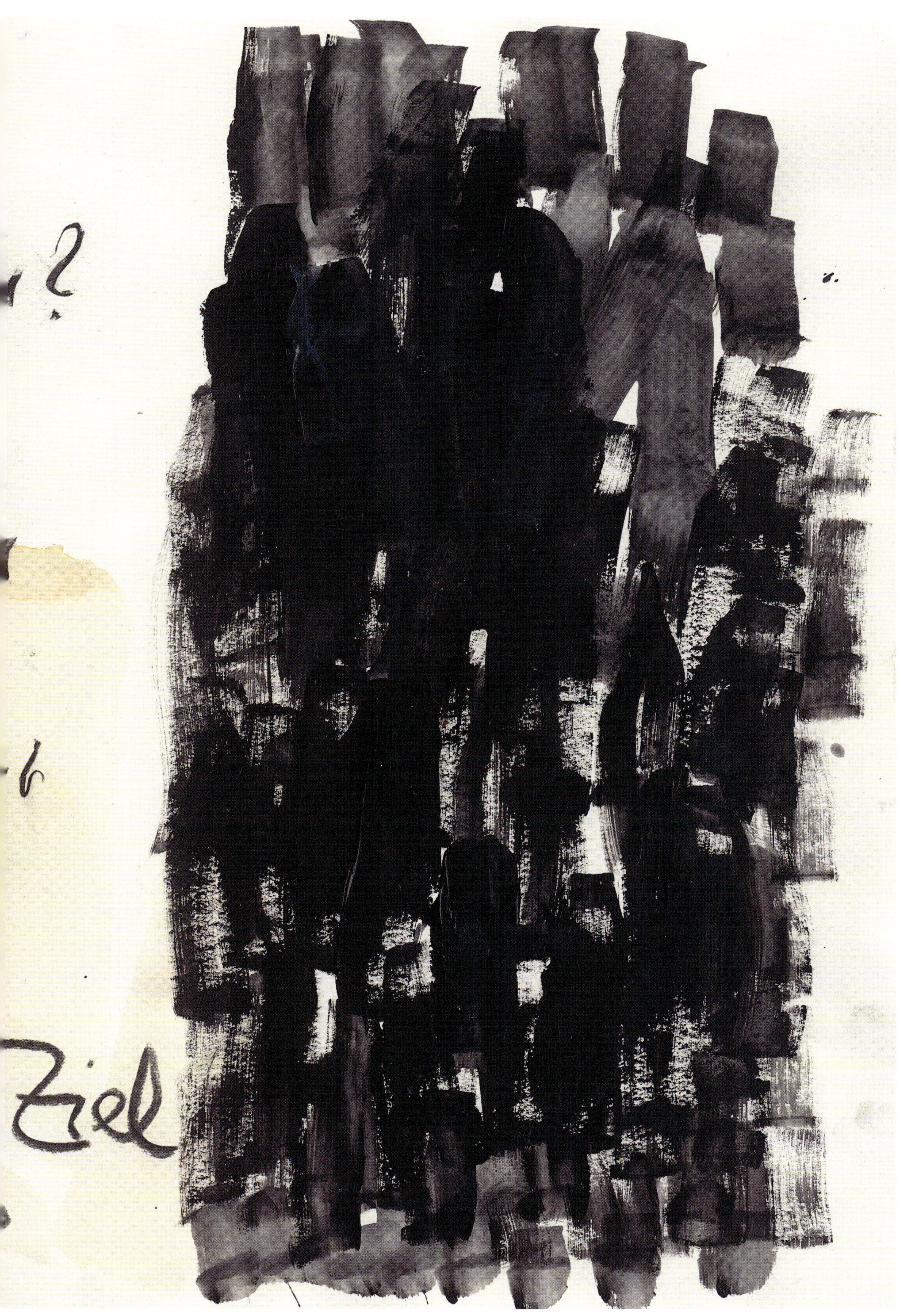

You can't hit me / I am off the hook / I'll just turn off my light / And then no moon no goal nada . . .

P.S.
____

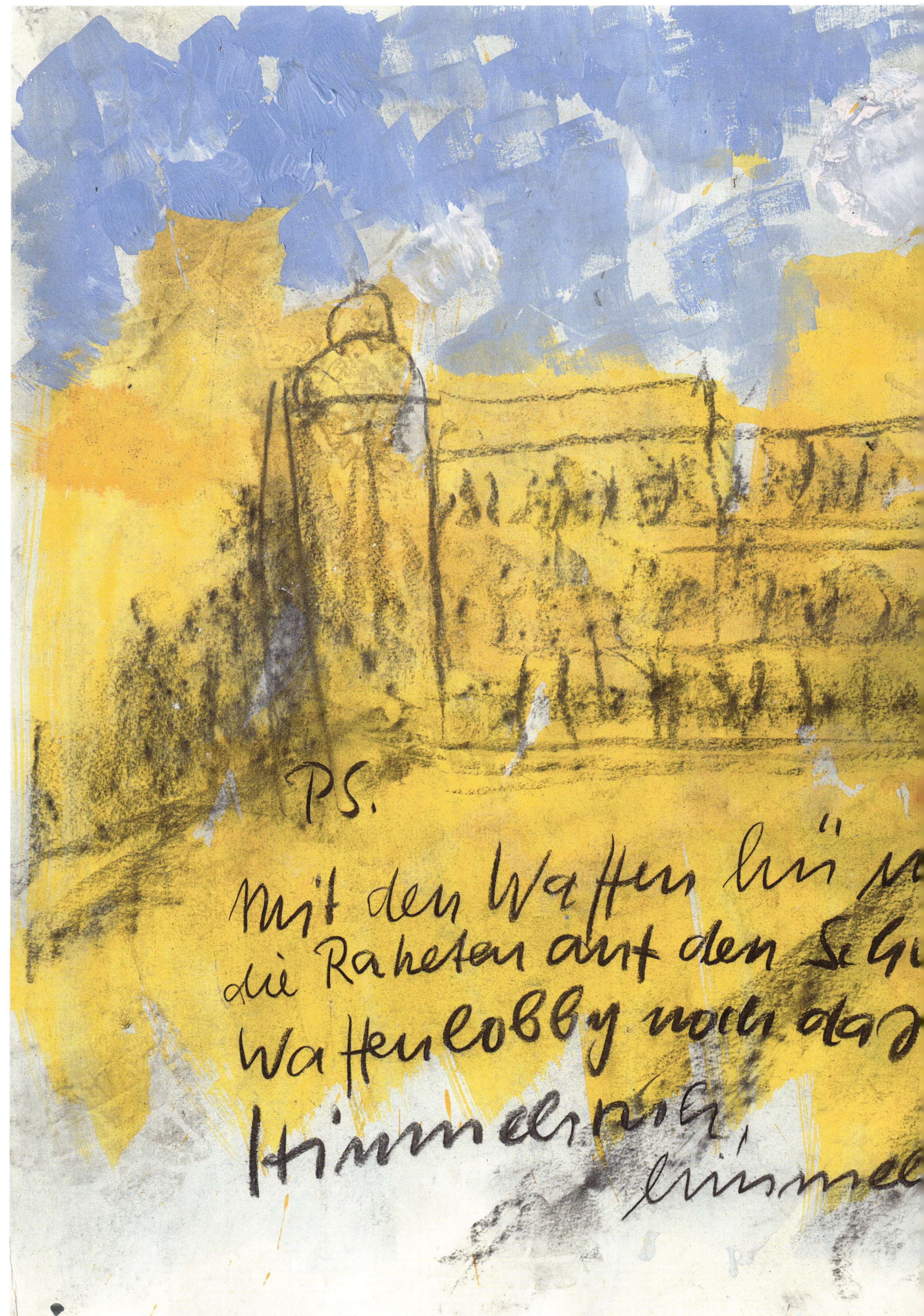

With the weapons / Giddyup / The rockets at the dump / The weapons' lobby a new lease /

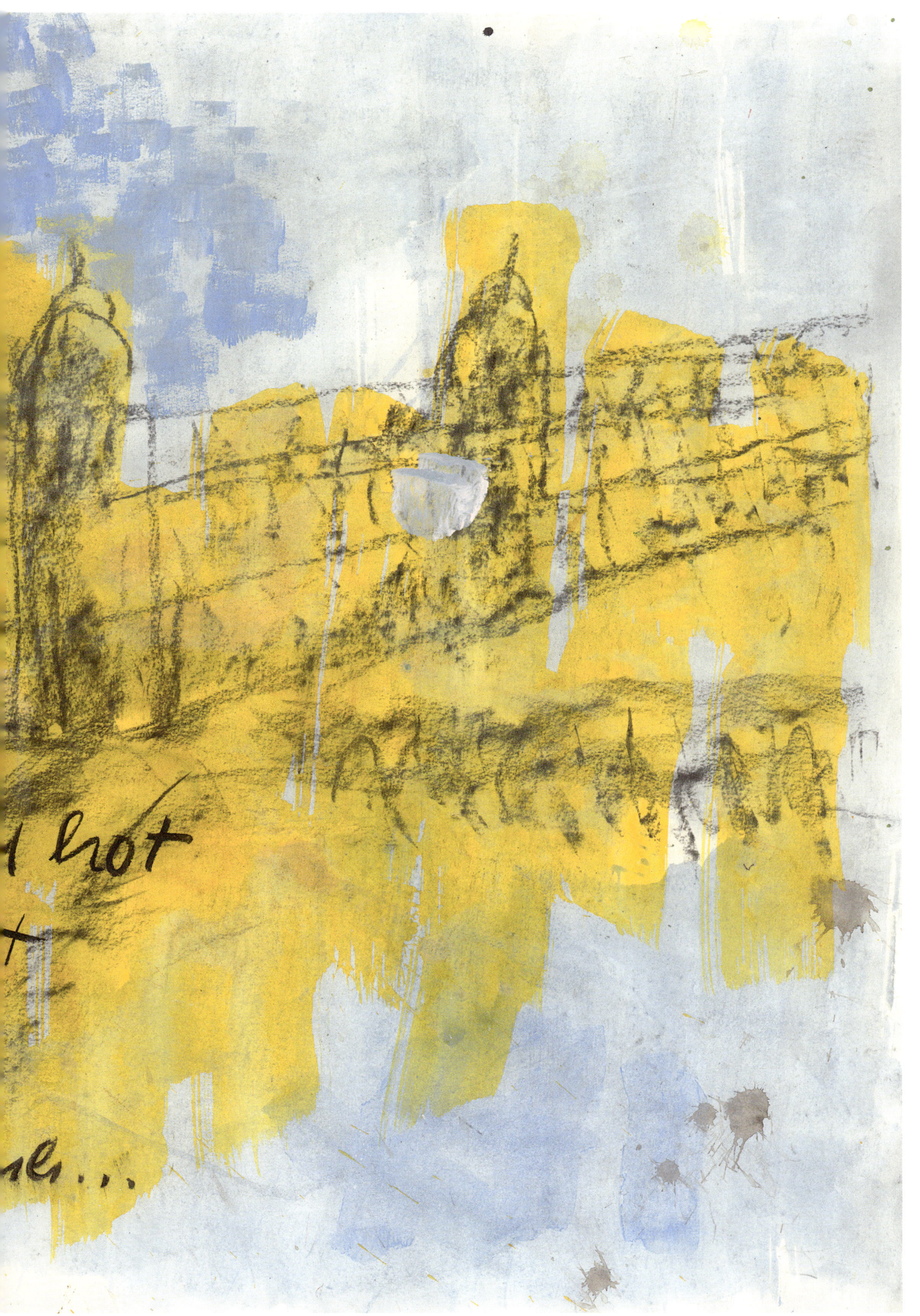

Heavenly peace . . . heavenly peace . . .

List of Illustrations

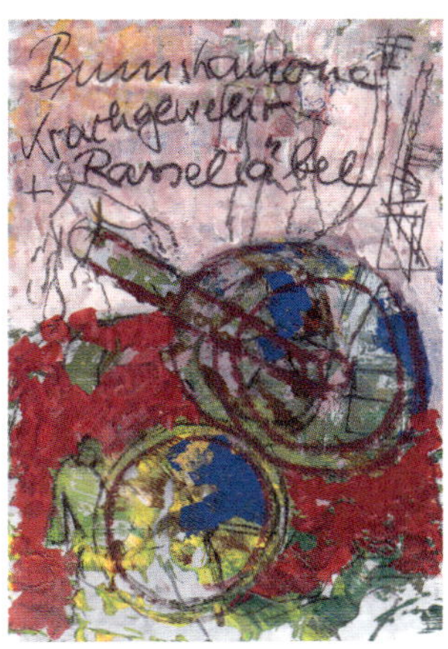

Page 6
*Bumskanone, Rasselsäbel
und Krachgewehr*
(Rockets to the Moon)
Acrylic and colored pencil on
paper, 2019 | 83.5 x 59 cm

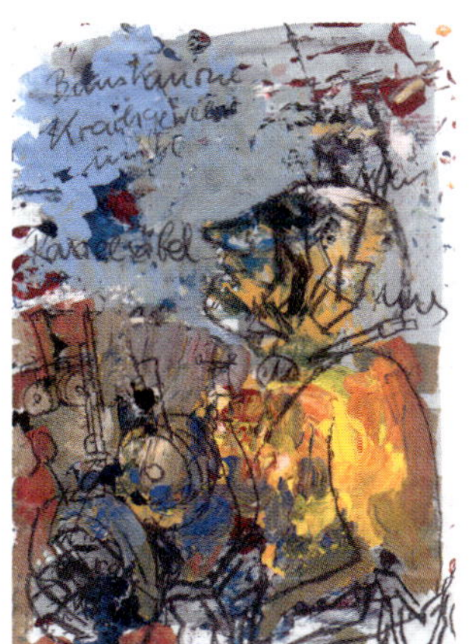

Page 15
*Bumskanone, Rasselsäbel
und Krachgewehr*
(Rockets to the Moon)
Acrylic and colored pencil on
paper, 2019 | 83.5 x 59 cm

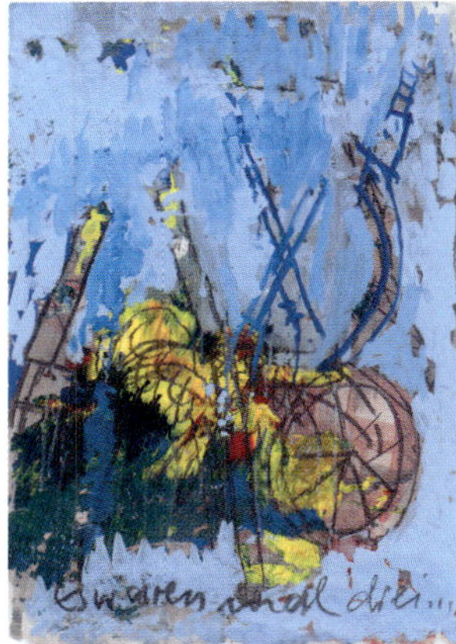

Page 17
*Es waren mal drei Waffen
(Once there were three
weapons)*
Acrylic and colored pencil on
paper, 2019 | 83.5 x 59 cm

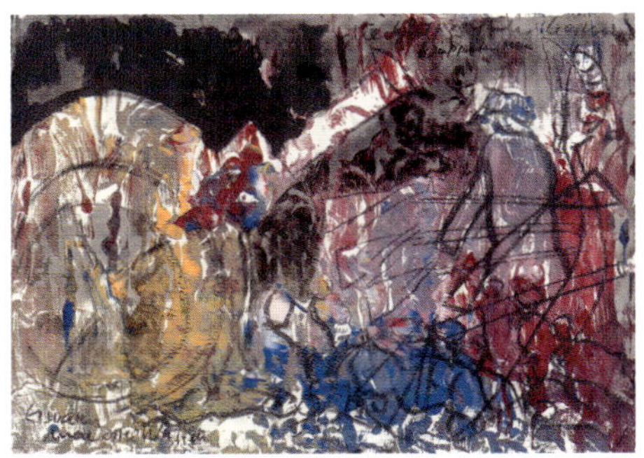

Pages 18/19
Die klapperten herum
(Just rattling around)
Acrylic and colored pencil on
paper, 2019 | 70 x 100 cm

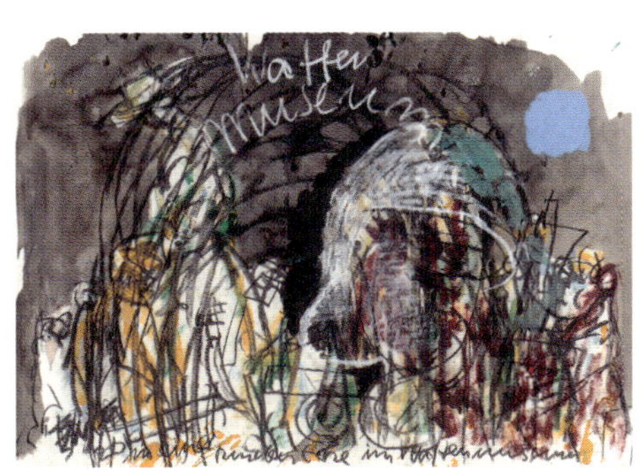

Pages 20/21
*In einer dunklen Ecke
Im Waffenmuseum*
**(Deep in a darkened corner
In the museum in town)**
Acrylic and colored pencil on
paper, 2019 | 70 x 100 cm

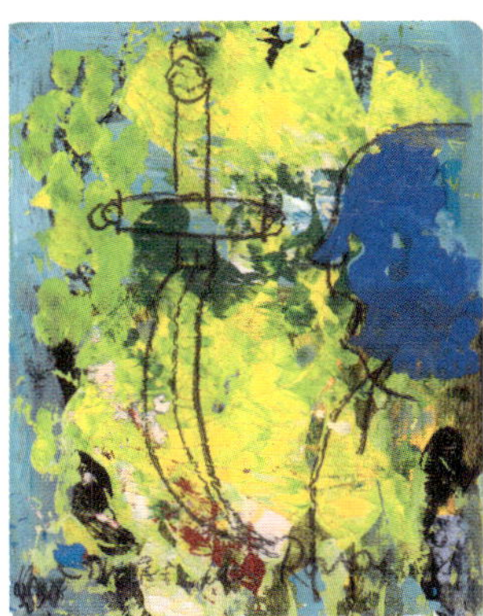

Page 23
Es war der Rasselsäbel
(It was the rattling saber)
Acrylic and colored pencil on
paper, 2019 | 60.5 x 48,2 cm

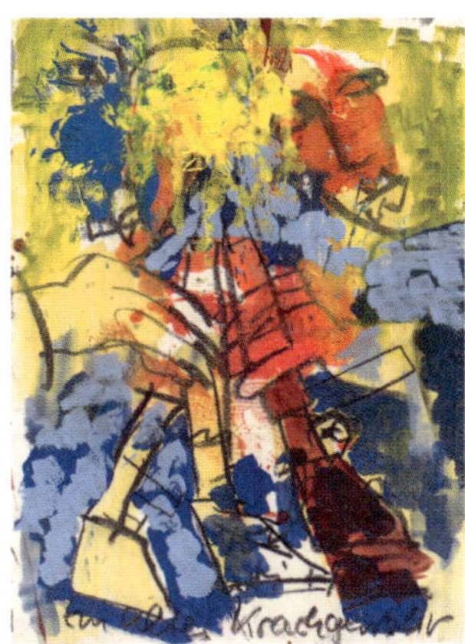

Page 25
Ein altes Krachgewehr
(Plus an old grenade one heard)
Acrylic and colored pencil on
paper, 2019 | 76 x 56 cm

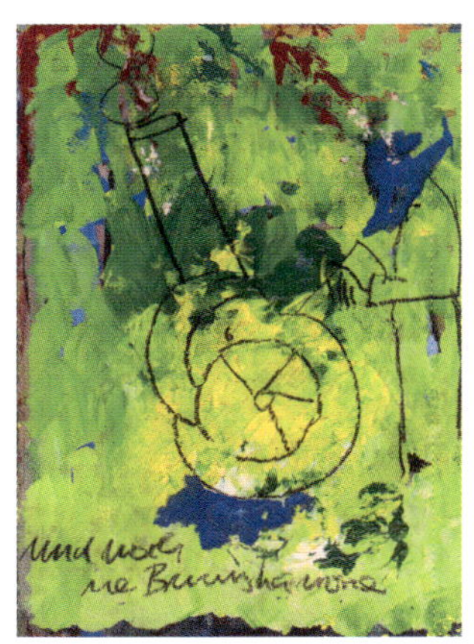

Page 27
Und noch ne Bumskanone
(And a large booming cannon)
Acrylic and colored pencil on
paper, 2019 | 76 x 56 cm

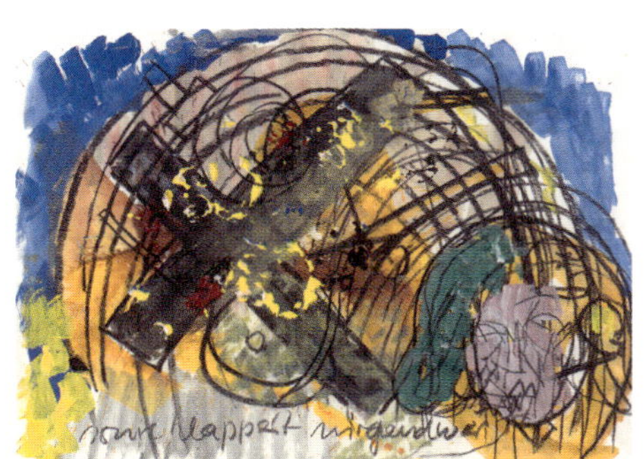

Pages 28/29
Sonst klappert nirgendwer
(Who all put in a word)
Acrylic and colored pencil on
paper, 2019 | 70 x 100 cm

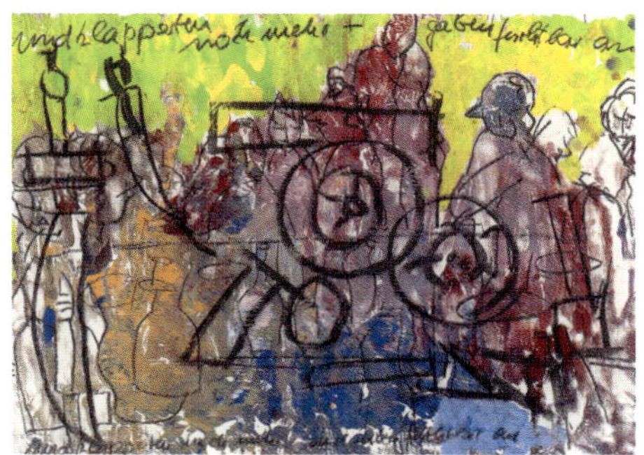

Pages 30/31
Und klapperten noch mehr
Und gaben furchtbar an
(And they rattled on and on
And bragged so puffed with air)
Acrylic and colored pencil on
paper, 2019 | 70 x 100 cm

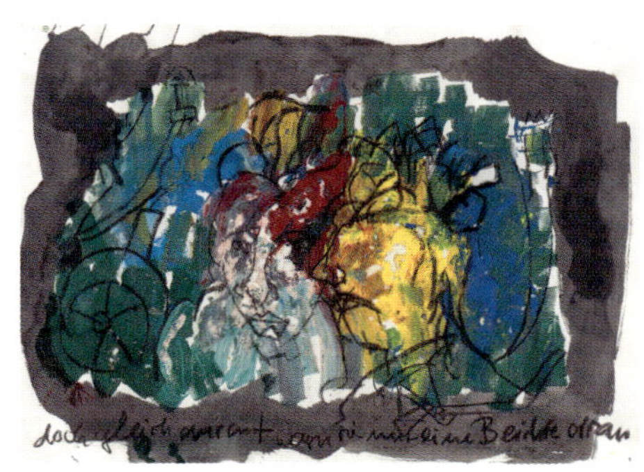

Pages 32/33
Doch gleich danach warn sie
Mit einer Beichte dran
(But shortly afterwards
They confessed—of sins aware)
Acrylic and colored pencil on
paper, 2019 | 70 x 100 cm

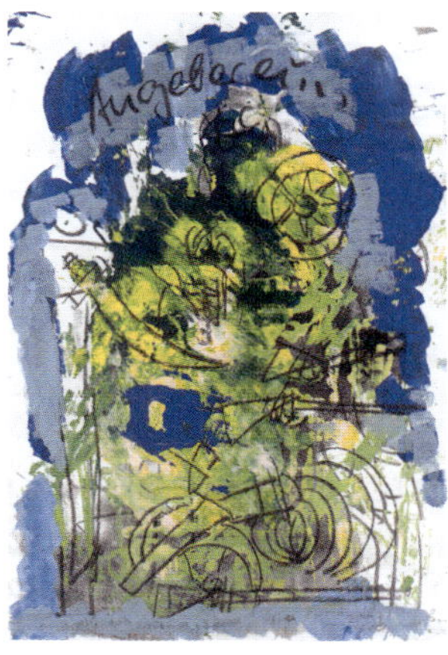

Page 35
Angeberei
(Bragging)
Acrylic and colored pencil on
paper, 2019 | 83.5 x 59 cm

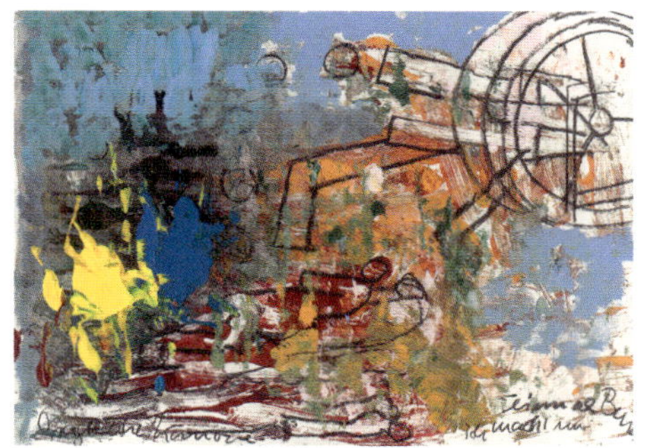

Pages 36/37
O sagte die Kanone
Ich macht nur einmal bum
(Oh said the cannon proud
I needed only once to boom)
Acrylic and colored pencil on
paper, 2019 | 70 x 100 cm

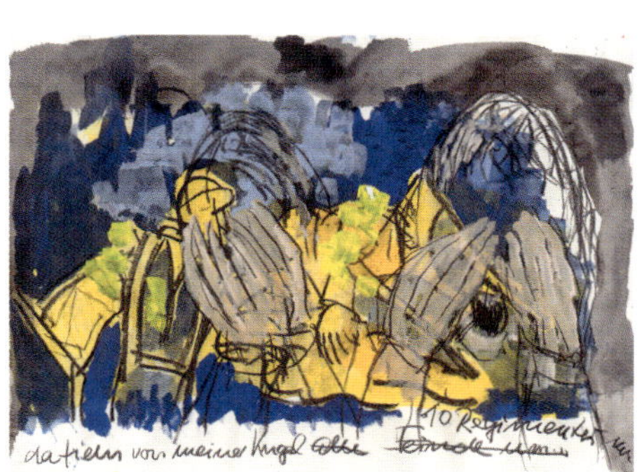

Pages 38/39
Da fieln von meiner Kugel
Zehn Regimenter um
(And with only one large cannon ball
Ten regiments met their doom)
Acrylic and colored pencil on
paper, 2019 | 70 x 100 cm

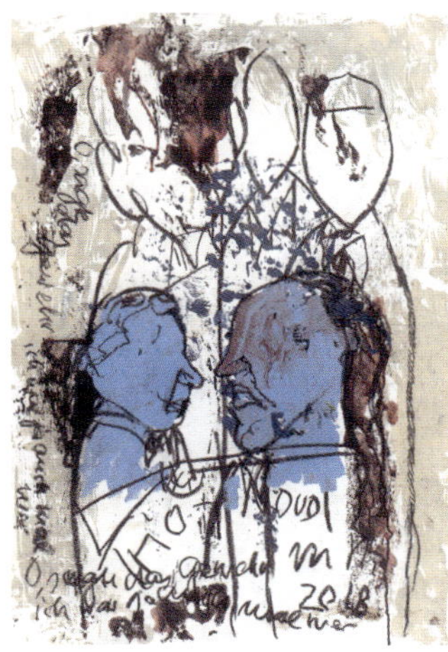

Page 41
O sagte das Gewehr
Ich war ja auch mal wer
(O said the rifle
I too was proud of dupes)
Acrylic and colored pencil on
paper, 2019 | 100 x 70 cm

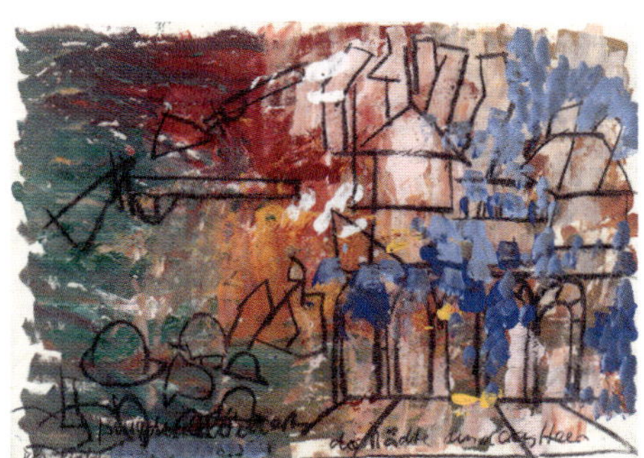

Pages 42/43
Ich habe peng durchlöchert
Das Stadt und noch das Heer
(I shot peng full of holes
The city and its troops)
Acrylic and colored pencil on
paper, 2019 | 70 x 100 cm

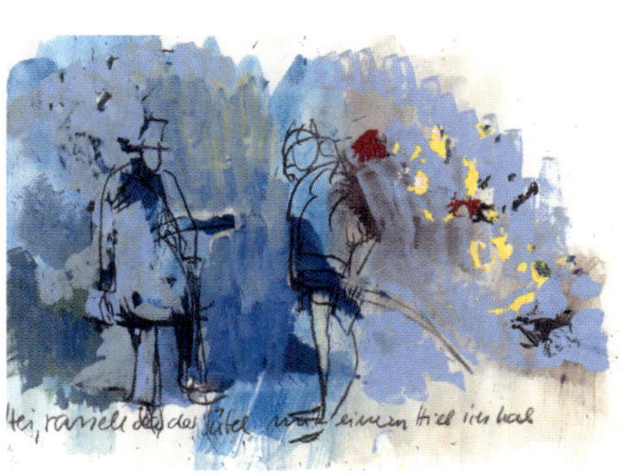

Pages 44/45
Hei rasselt da der Säbel
Mit einem Hieb ich hab
(Hey returned the saber
With one fell swoop did I)
Acrylic and colored pencil on
paper, 2019 | 70 x 100 cm

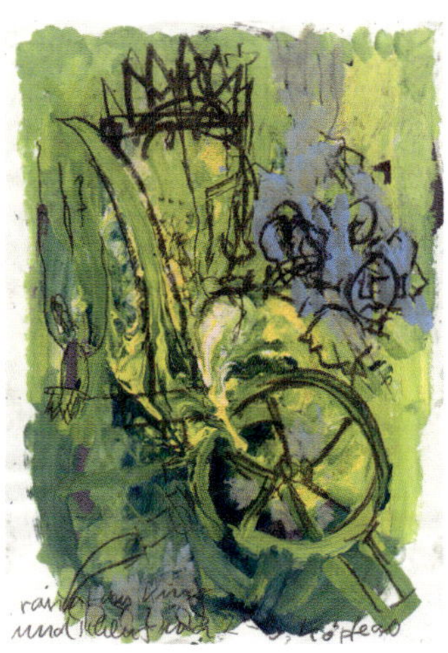

Page 47
Rasiert den King und schlug /
Noch zwei drei Köpfe ab
(Mow down the king and with one strike
Several heads did fly)
Acrylic and colored pencil on paper,
2019 | 85.5 x 61 cm

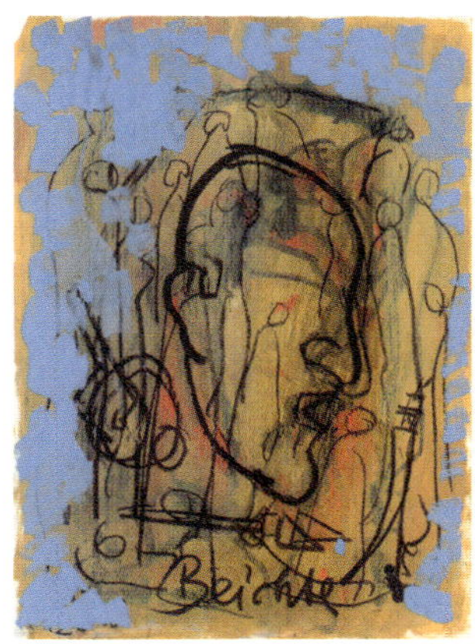

Page 49
Beichte
(Confession)
Acrylic and colored pencil on
paper, 2019 | 76 x 56.5 cm

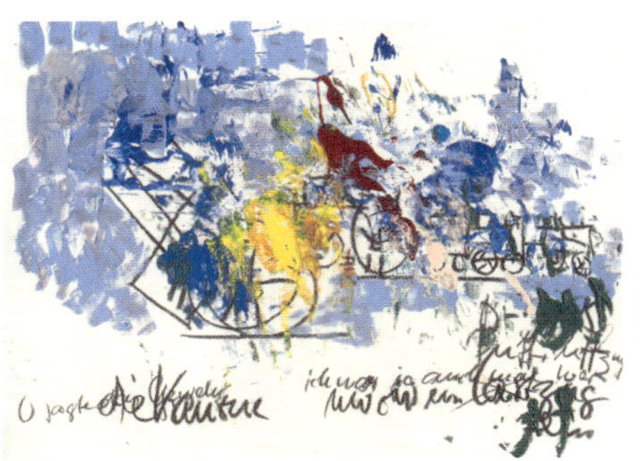

Pages 50/51
O sagte die Kanone
Ich möcht ein D-Zug sein
(O said the cannon proud
I wish I were a train)
Acrylic and colored pencil on
paper, 2019 | 70 x 100 cm

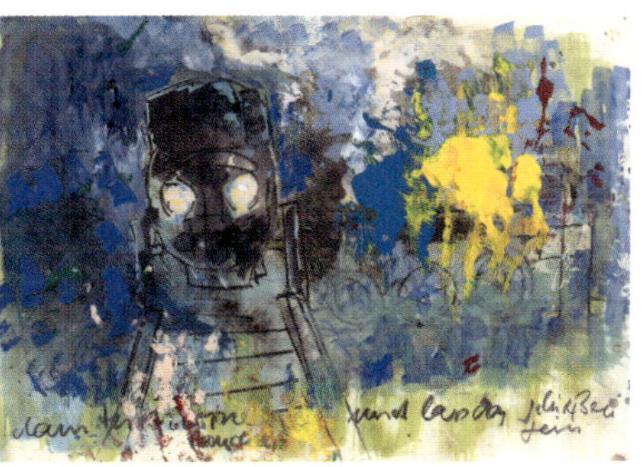

Pages 52/53
Dann tu ich vorne rauchen
Und lass das schießen sein
(Then I would smoke away up front
And halt my shooting brain)
Acrylic and colored pencil on paper,
2019 | 70 x 100 cm

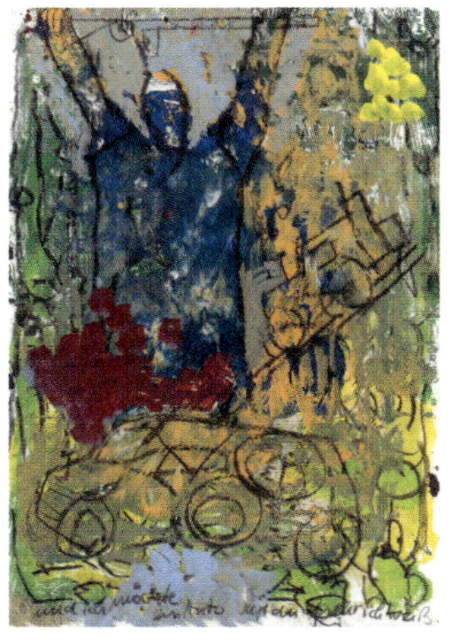

Page 55
Und ich möchte ein Auto
Sagt das Gewehr ich weiß
(Or an auto I would like to be
Said the rifle then I'd know)
Acrylic and colored pencil on
paper, 2019 | 100 x 70 cm

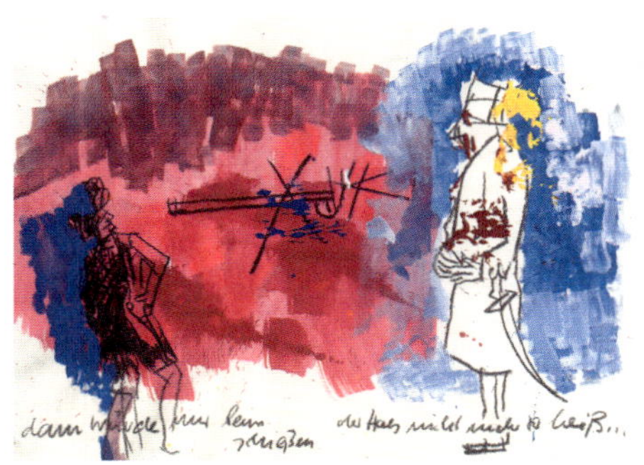

Pages 56/57
Dann würde mir beim Schießen
Der Hals nicht mehr so heiß
(That when I'd be a' shooting
My neck wouldn't hurt me so)
Acrylic and colored pencil on
paper, 2019 | 70 x 100 cm

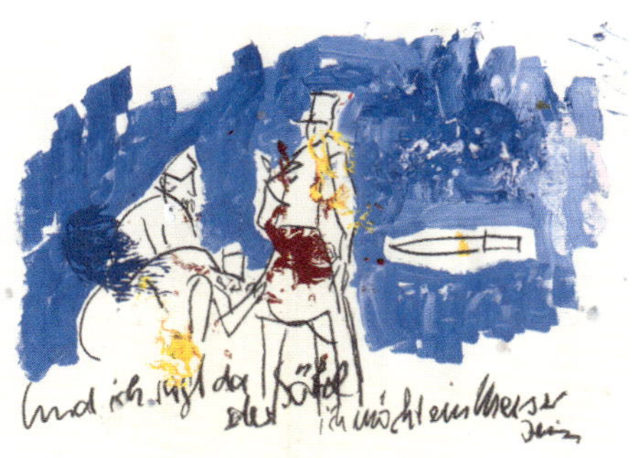

Pages 58/59
Und ich sagt da der Säbel
Ich möcht ein Messer sein
(And I said the saber
I'd like to be a knife)
Acrylic and colored pencil on
paper, 2019 | 70 x 100 cm

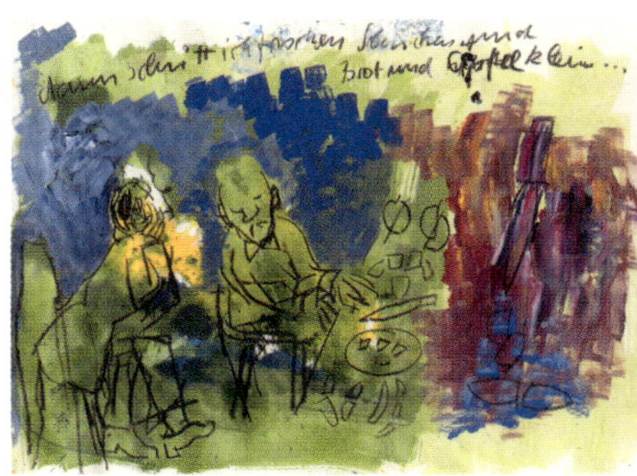

Pages 60/61
Dann schnitt ich frischen Schinken
Und Brot und Äpfel klein
(I'd cut some ham and bread and apples
And be happy with my life)
Acrylic and colored pencil on paper,
2019 | 100 x 70 cm

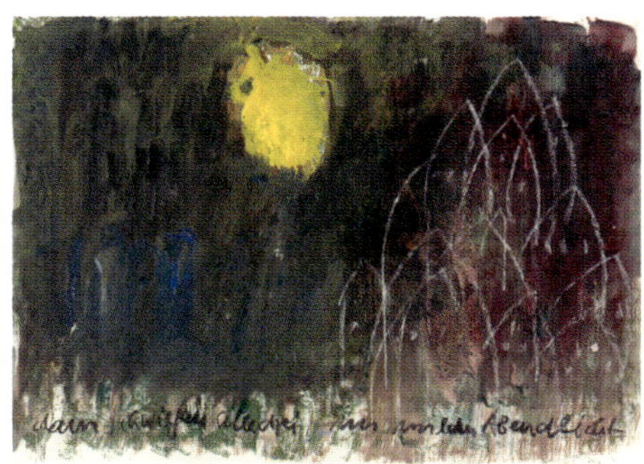

Pages 62/63
Dann schwiegen alle drei
Im milden Abendlicht
(Then all the three fell silent
In the mild evening light)
Acrylic and colored pencil on
paper, 2019 | 70 x 100 cm

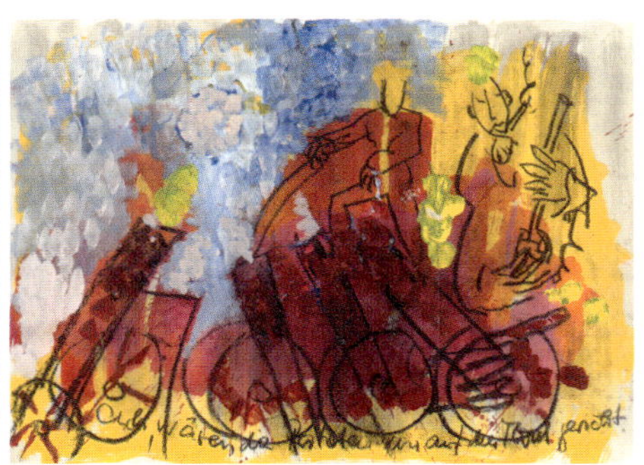

Pages 64/65
Ach wären die Raketen
Nur auf den Mond gerichtet
(If only the rockets there
Had been shot at the moon so bright)
Acrylic and colored pencil on
paper, 2019 | 70 x 100 cm

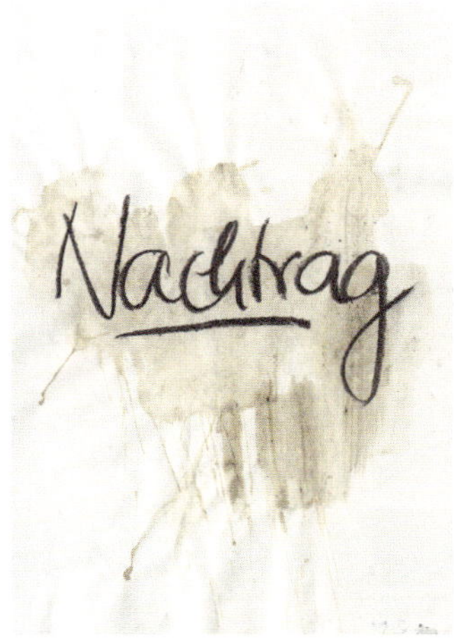

Page 67
Nachtrag
(Postscript)
Acrylic and colored pencil on
paper, 2019 | 59.5 x 42 cm

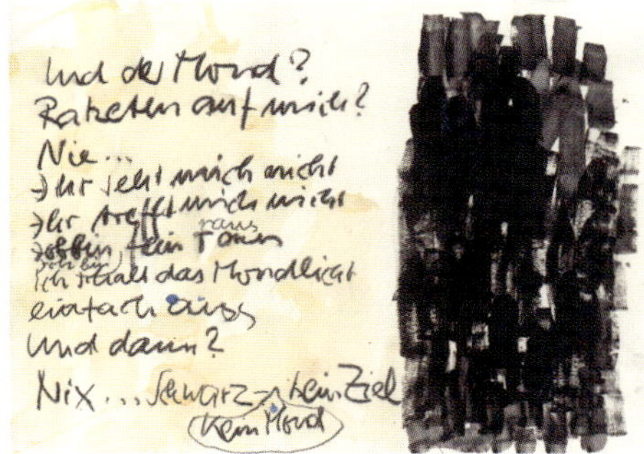

Pages 68/69
Und der Mond?
Raketen auf mich? Seid ihr noch bei Sinnen?
Ihr seht mich nicht
Ihr trefft mich nicht
Ich bin fein raus
Ich schalt das Mondlicht
Einfach aus
Und dann
Kein Mond, kein Ziel, nix …
(And the moon?
Rockets at me? Are you all nuts?
You see me not
You can't hit me
I am off the hook
I'll just turn off my light
And then no moon no goal nada . . .)
Acrylic and colored pencil on paper,
2019 | 70 x 100 cm

Page 71
PS.
(P.S.)
Acrylic and colored pencil on
paper, 2019 | 59.5 x 42 cm

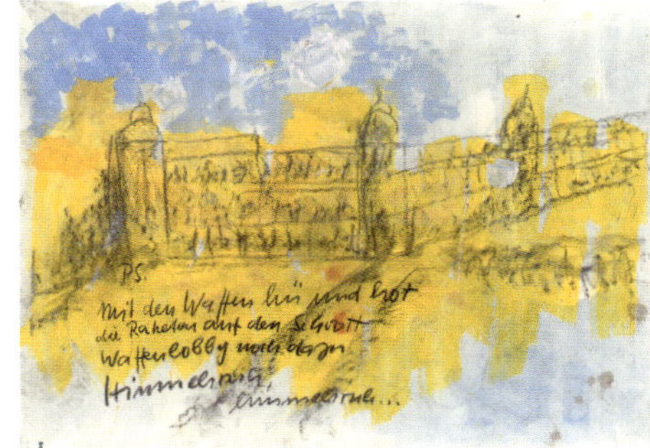

Pages 72/73
Mit den Waffen hü und hott
Die Raketen auf den Schrott
Die Waffenlobby noch dazu
Himmelsruh … Himmelsruh …
(With the weapons
Giddyup
The rockets at the dump
The weapons' lobby a new lease
Heavenly peace . . . heavenly peace . . .)
Acrylic and colored pencil on paper,
2019 | 70 x 100 cm

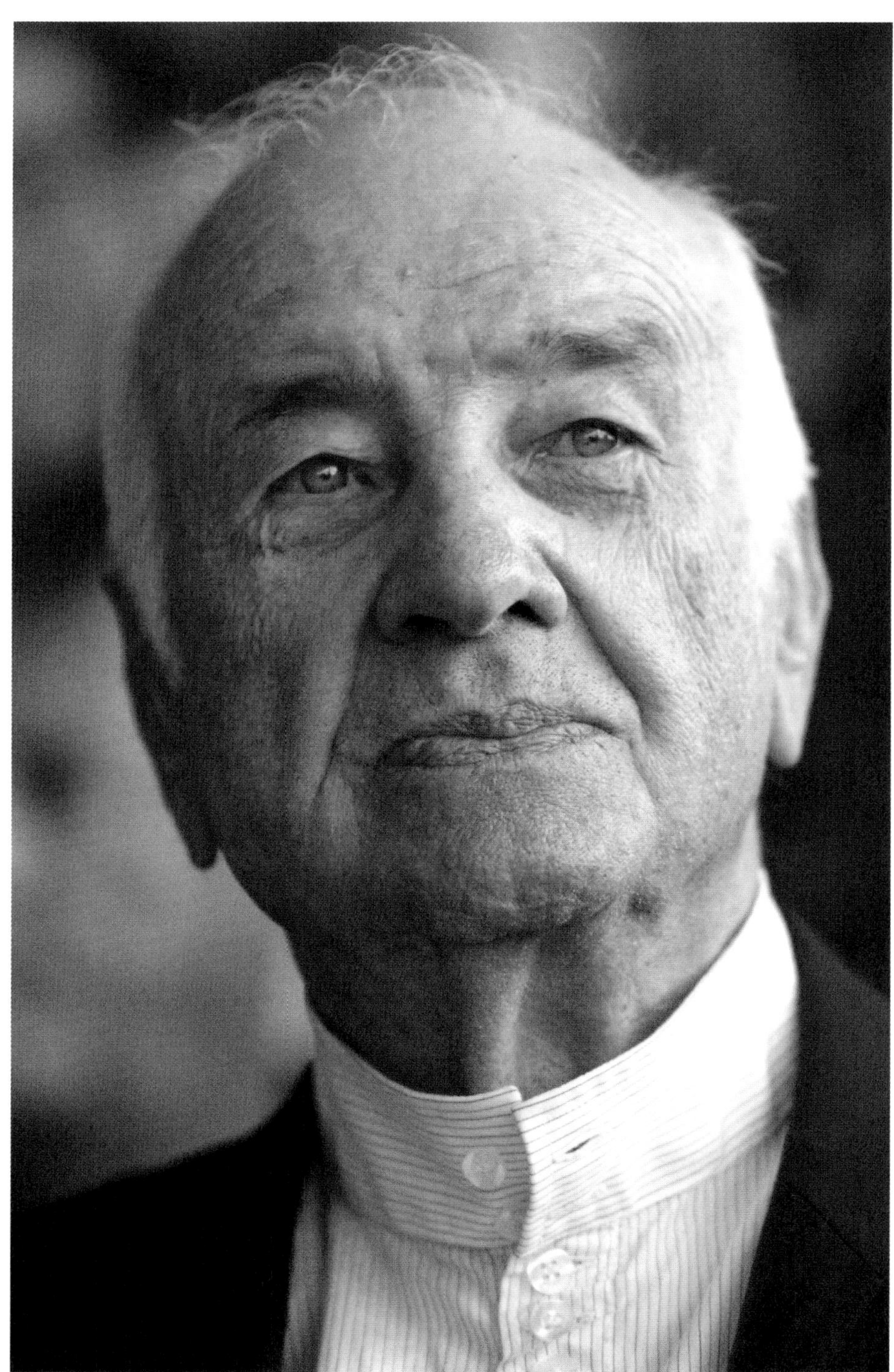

Biography

Born December 17, 1930
· Born in Tilsit, East Prussia (now Sovetsk, Russia)

1949
· Studies music at the Stern'schen Konservatorium, Berlin

1951
· Acting lessons and turns to painting

1952
· Theater am Schiffbauerdamm, Berlin

1953
· Completes music studies at the Volksbühne in Berlin

1956
· First role in a feature film, *Heimliche Ehen* (Secret Marriages)

1959–60
· Theater, television, and cinema in the German Democratic Republic (GDR)

1963
· Kunstpreis der DDR (Art Prize of the GDR)

1964–65
· Silberner Lorbeer (Silver Laurel) of DDR-Fernsehfunk (GDR Broadcasting) for the role of Wolfgang Pagel in *Wolf unter Wölfen* (Wolf among Wolves)

1967–68
· Concert tours to Copenhagen, Vienna, Warsaw, Cairo, West Berlin

1972
· Nationalpreis zweiter Klasse (National Prize, Second Class) of the GDR for *Die Verschworenen* (The Conspirators)

1975
· Theodor-Körner-Preis (for the ensemble) for his role as a Stasi agent in *Das unsichtbare Visier* (The Invisible Visor)

1976
· Signs resolution by GDR artists protesting Wolf Biermann being deprived of his GDR citizenship

1979
· Emigrates from the GDR; first roles in West Germany

1980
· Verdienstkreuz erster Klasse (Cross of Merit, First Class) of the Federal Republic of Germany

1981
· Publication of his first novel, *Verordneter Sonntag* (Decreed Sunday), Severin und Siedler Verlag, Berlin

1982
· Bundesfilmpreis (Filmband in Gold) (Federal Film Prize [Film Strip in Gold]) for his role as Bohm in Rainer Werner Fassbinder's *Lola*

1983
· Deutscher Darstellerpreis "Chaplin-Schuh" (German Actors' Prize "Chaplin Shoe")

1985
· Prize for Best Actor of the Festival des films du monde de Montréal for the role of the farmer Leon in *Bittere Ernte (Angry Harvest)*
· Bundesfilmpreis (Filmband in Gold) (Federal Film Prize [Film Strip in Gold]) for the film *Oberst Redl (Colonel Redl)*
· Invited to Los Angeles by the Hollywood agent Paul Kohner

1991
· Publication of his book Drehtage: *"Music Box" und "Avalon,"* (Shooting Days: "Music Box" and "Avalon") Luchterhand Verlag, Frankfurt am Main

1992
· Moves to the United States (Los Angeles, Marina del Rey)

- Silberner Bär (Silver Bear) for playing Baron
  Kaspar von Utz in *Utz*
- Views his own Stasi files at the Stasi Records
  Agency in Berlin

1996
- Golden Satellite for the role of Peter Helfgott
  in *Shine*
- AACTA (Australian Academy of Cinema and
  Television Arts) Award for best supporting
  actor in *Shine*

1997
- Publication of his memoirs *Unterwegs nach
  Hause* (Homebound), Aufbau Verlag, Berlin
- Oscar nomination for his role as Peter
  Helfgott in *Shine*
- Awarded the Berlinale-Kamera for his
  lifework

1998
- Honorary doctorate from Spertus Institute
  for Jewish Studies in Chicago
- Publication of his novel *In Gedanken an Marie
  Louise* (In Memory of Marie Louise), List
  Verlag, Munich

2001–2002
- Publication of his book *Rollenspiel: Texte und
  Malerei; ein während der Dreharbeiten zu "Die
  Manns" geführtes Tagebuch* (Role-Play: Texts
  and Painting: A Diary during the Shooting of
  "Die Manns"), Strauss Verlag, Potsdam
- First lithographs, at the suggestion of the
  gallery owner Frank-Thomas Gaulin,
  Kunsthaus Lübeck
- Individual lithographs on the subject
  "Biographical Worlds of Images"
- Portfolio *Hamlet in Amerika*, thirteen
  lithographs on a copy of one the actor's
  scripts, Kunsthaus Lübeck
- Grimme-Preis mit Gold (Grimme Prize with
  Gold) for playing Thomas Mann in *Die Manns:
  Ein Jahrhundertroman* (The Manns: A Novel of
  the Century)
- Bayerischer Filmpreis (Bavarian Film Prize)
  for playing Thomas Mann in *Die Manns: Ein
  Jahrhundertroman*

- Emmy Award in New York for *Die Manns: Ein
  Jahrhundertroman*
- Publication of the book *Armin Mueller-Stahl,
  Begegnungen* (Encounters) by Volker Skierka,
  Knesebeck Verlag, Munich
- Bundesverdienstkreuz (Cross of Merit)

2003
- Portfolio of twenty large-format lithographs
  on *Urfaust* (with catalogue), Kunsthaus
  Lübeck

2004
- Portfolio *Night on Earth—Day on Earth*, cycle
  with twenty-one lithographs on the film
  Night on Earth by Jim Jarmusch (with
  catalogue), Kunsthaus Lübeck
- Four of his graphic portfolios are added to the
  collection of the Landesmuseum für Kunst-
  und Kulturgeschichte Schloss Gottorf,
  Schleswig
- Grosses Verdienstkreuz der Bundesrepublik
  Deutschland (Grand Cross of Merit of the
  Federal Republic of Germany)

2005
- kultur aktuell prize of the HSH-Nordbank
  and the Landeskulturverband Schleswig-
  Holstein for his graphic oeuvre
- DEFA-Stiftung prize for his contributions to
  German film
- Publication of his book *Venice – Ein amerika-
  nisches Tagebuch*, Aufbau Verlag, Berlin

2006
- Awarded the Carl-Zuckmayer-Medaille of the
  State of the Rhineland-Palatinate
- Publication of his book *Kettenkarussell*
  (Chain Carousel), Aufbau Verlag, Berlin
- Publication of his book *Unterwegs nach Hause*
  (Homebound), Aufbau Verlag, Berlin
- Publication of his book *Portraits*, Aufbau
  Verlag, Berlin

2007
- Awarded the Deutscher Filmpreis
  (Honorary Award for Outstanding
  Contributions to German Cinema)

- Awarded the Bild Osgar
- Designs an artist's edition of the Brockhaus encyclopedia
- Film *Die Buddenbrooks*
- Publication of his book Die Buddenbrooks: *Übermalungen eines Drehbuchs* (Overpaintings of a Screenplay), Henschel Verlag, Berlin
- Publication of his book *Hannah*, Aufbau Verlag, Berlin
- Publication of his book *Utz*, Braus Verlag, Berlin

2008
- Grosses Bundesverdienstkreuz mit Stern (Grand Cross of Merit with Star)
- Genie Award of the Academy of Canadian Cinema and Television ("Canadian Oscar") as bester supporting actor in *Tödliche Versprechen* (*Eastern Promises*)

2009
- Award in honor of his lifework, Berlinale Berlin

2010
- Landesverdienstorden (State Orders of Merit) of the State of North Rhine-Westphalia
- Publication of his book *Die Jahre werden schneller: Lieder und Gedichte* (The Years Are Getting Faster: Songs and Poems), Aufbau Verlag, Berlin
- Monograph *Armin Mueller-Stahl: Werkmonografie, Malerei und Zeichnungen* (Monograph on His Oeuvre of Paintings and Drawings), Edition Braus, Berlin
- *Armin Mueller-Stahl: Die Biografie*, by Gabriele Michel, Aufbau Verlag, Berlin
- *Armin Mueller-Stahl: Die Biografie*, by Volker Skierka, Langen/Müller Verlag, Munich
- Honorary citizen of the State of Schleswig-Holstein

2011
- Honorary citizen of the city of Sovetsk (formerly Tilsit)
- Honorary Fellowship for Painting at the Villa Massimo, Rome
- Goldene Kamera for his lifework

- Bambi for his lifework
- Goldener Bär (Golden Bear) for his lifework

2013
- Platin-Romy for his lifework, Vienna
- Europäischer Kulturpreis Pro Arte
- Europäischer Kunst- und Filmbiennale-Preis, Worpswede

2014
- Honorary prize of the thirty-fifth Bayerischer Filmpreis (Bavarian Film Prize)
- Askania Award 2014
- Lifetime Achievement Award, Portland German Film Festival
- Honorary Leopard Award for his lifework, sixty-seventh Locarno Film Festival
- Publication of his book *Dreimal Deutschland und zurück* (Three Times to Germany and Back). Biographical narrative, written down by Andreas Hallaschka, Verlag Hoffmann und Campe, Hamburg

2015
- *Arbeiten auf Papier / Works on Paper*, Hatje Cantz Verlag, Berlin

2016
- The Washington Jewish Film Festival: Visionary Award
- Deutscher Schauspielerpreis (German Actors' Prize): honor for his lifework
- Publication of his book *Die Blaue Kuh* (The Blue Cow), Hatje Cantz Verlag, Berlin

2018
- Portfolio *Shakespeares Mädchen und Frauen* (Shakespeare's Girls and Women), Kunsthaus Lübeck
- Publication of his book Der wien *Vogel fliegen kann* (He Who Can Fly Like a Bird), Hatje Cantz Verlag, Berlin

2019
- Prize of the Dresdner Opernball, St. Petersburg

Solo Exhibitions (Selection)

2001
- First exhibition of paintings and drawings, Filmmuseum, Potsdam
- Buddenbrookhaus und Kulturforum Museum Burgkloster, Lübeck, Kunsthaus Lübeck (with catalogue)
- Büchergilde Gutenberg, Bremen
- Solo exhibition of paintings and drawings, Galerie Rolf Kallenbach, Munich

2002
- *Von Durban nach Dubai auf der MS Europa* (From Durban to Dubai on the MS Europa), Galerie Rolf Kallenbach, Munich

2003
- Kulturhistorisches Museum, Stralsund
- Galerie Börges, Bremerhaven
- Stadt- und Industriemuseum and Galerie am Dom, Wetzlar
- Rathaus Wallenhorst
- *Festival Mitte Europa*, Städtische Galerie e. o. plauen, Plauen

2004
- Kunstraum Akademie, Stuttgart
- Casa di Goethe, Rome
- Wenzel Hablik Museum, Itzehoe
- Landesmuseum für Kunst- und Kulturgeschichte Schloss Gottorf, Schleswig
- Kulturbund Altenburger Land, Altenburg
- Galerie Abrahams, Hamburg
- Heidelberger Kunstverein

2005
- Los Angeles Municipal Art Gallery, Barnsdall Art Park
- Manus Presse, Stuttgart
- Herzog August Bibliothek, Wolfenbüttel
- Ostholstein-Museum, Eutin (with catalogue)
- Kunsthalle Kühlungsborn

2006
- *Urfaust* series, Museum der bildenden Künste, Leipzig
- Kunstverein "Talstrasse" e. V., Halle
- Museen der Stadt Meiningen (with catalogue)
- Series of graphic works, Kunsthaus Lübeck
- Museum Schloss Güstrow (with catalogue)

2007
- Museum für Kunst und Gewerbe, Hamburg, on the book *Utz*
- Kunsthalle Mannheim
- Theatergalerie Bremen (with catalogue)
- Kunstforum Altes Rathaus, Potsdam (with catalogue)
- Art Karlsruhe One-artist-show, Kunsthaus Lübeck

2008
- Galerie umĕni Karlovy Vary, Czech Republic (with catalogue)
- Kunststation Kleinsassen, Hofbieber-Kleinsassen / Rhön (with catalogue)
- Landesmuseum für Kunst- und Kulturgeschichte Schloss Gottorf, Schleswig (Internationaler Museumstag)
- Frank-Loebsches-Haus, Landau in der Pfalz (with catalogue)
- Kunstverein Wasgau, Dahn
- Art Karlsruhe, Kunsthaus Lübeck

2009
- Museum Schloss Burgk
- Weidener Kulturtage
- Landesmuseum für Kunst- und Kulturgeschichte Schloss Gottorf, Schleswig
- Kunstverein Geldern
- Städtisches Museum, Göttingen
- NRW-Forum Düsseldorf
- Galerie Ketterer, Munich
- Horst-Janssen-Museum, Oldenburg

- Sparkassenstiftung Schleswig-Holstein, Kiel
(with catalogue *Ars borealis*)
- Kunstverein Peschkenhaus, Moers

2010
- Baden-Württembergische Bank, Stuttgart
- Art Karlsruhe One-artist-show, Kunsthaus
Lübeck
- Ostholstein-Museum, Eutin (with catalogue)
- Städtische Galerie "Leerer Beutel,"
Regensburg (with catalogue)
- Schloss Wackerbarth, Radebeul
- Museum of the History of the Town of
Sovetsk (formerly Tilsit)
- Kunsthalle Ammersee, Seefeld
- "spinart," One-artist-show of paintings,
Kunsthaus Lübeck at the Baumwollspinnerei
Leipzig
- Town of Neumarkt in der Oberpfalz and
Galerie Herrmann
- Kunsthalle Kühlungsborn

2011
- Exhibition in the Landtag (State Parliament)
of Schleswig-Holstein
- Galerie am Dom, Wetzlar
- Kunstverein Villa Böhm, Neustadt an der
Weinstrasse (with catalogue)
- Galerie der Braunschweigischen
Landessparkasse, Braunschweig
- Galerie Thomas Kaphammel, Braunschweig
- Kunstverein Dissen
- Art Karlsruhe One-artist-show, Kunsthaus
Lübeck
- Kunstraum Potsdam / Filmmuseum Potsdam
two-person exhibition with Jürgen Böttcher-
Strawalde (with catalogue)

2012
- Stiftung Burg Kniphausen, Burg Kniphausen,
Wilhelmshaven (with catalogue)
- VW-Forum unter den Linden, Berlin
(with catalogue)

- Art Karlsruhe One-artist-show, Kunsthaus
Lübeck
- Christian Hohmann Fine Art, Palm Desert,
Paintings, Works on Paper and Fine Prints
- Galerie Noah, Augsburg
- Kunstmuseum Solingen
- Marktkirche Goslar
- Galerie Anders, Lünen
- Siegfried Museum, Xanten with Kunsthandel
Koenen

2013
- Kulturkirche Neuruppin (with catalogue)
- Art Karlsruhe One-artist-show, Kunsthaus
Lübeck
- Kunsthaus Hänisch, Kappeln
- "Ballenlager" im Kulturzentrum Greven in
collaboration with Galerie Hunold
- Hanse-Office Brüssel (gemeinsame
Vertretung der Freien und Hansestadt
Hamburg und des Landes Schleswig-Holstein
bei der EU)
- Bruckner-Haus Linz (with catalogue)
- Kunststation Kleinsassen

2014
- Art Karlsruhe One-artist-show, Kunsthaus
Lübeck / Kunsthalle Schloss Seefeld, Bayern
- Galerie Herrmann and Kulturhaus Reitstadl,
Neumarkt
- Bikini-Haus, Gallery Weekend Berlin with
Hatje Cantz Verlag, Berlin
- Galerie Kersten, Brunnthal bei München
- Schloss Achberg, Ravensburg: group
exhibition with Margarita Broich, Günter
Grass, Udo Lindenberg, and Alissa Walser
(with catalogue)
- Kulturzentrum Kolvenburg Billerbeck, Kreis
Coesfeld
- Stadtmuseum Siegburg
- Kunsthalle Kühlungsborn
- Galerie im Taschenbergpalais, Dresden
- Galerie Bäumler, Regensburg

· Art Fair Köln One-artist-show

2015
· Art Karlsruhe, One-artist-show, Kunsthaus
  Lübeck
· Art Karlsruhe, One-artist-show, Kunsthalle
  Schloss Seefeld, Bayern
· Kunsthalle Brennabor, Brandenburg (with
  catalogue)
· Galerie Richter, Lütjenburg
· Galerie Peters-Barenbrock, Ahrenshoop
· Orangerie, Fürst-Pückler-Park, Bad Muskau
  (with catalogue)
· Fabrik der Künste, Hamburg
· Schleswig-Holstein-Haus, Schwerin
· Ostholstein-Museum, Eutin (with catalogue)

2016
· Art Karlsruhe, One-artist-show, Kunsthaus
  Lübeck
· Galerie Herrmann, Neumarkt
· Galerie Palz, Saarlouis
· Schloss Hartenfels, Torgau (with catalogue)
· Kreissparkasse Heilbronn (with catalogue) /
  Galerie Nupnau Art & Photographie,
  Schwaigern
· art + form, Dresden
· Galerie Walentowski, Werl
· Galerie Z, Landau
· Ernst Ludwig Kirchner Verein, Fehmarn

2017
· Art Karlsruhe, One-artist-show, Kunsthaus
  Lübeck
· Dokumentationszentrum Prora in
  collaboration with Kunstraum Wasserwerk,
  Rügen
· Salongalerie "Die Möwe" Berlin
· Osthaus Museum Hagen (with catalogue)
· Stadtmuseum Amberg
· Galerie am Dom, Wetzlar – Stadt-Galerie im
  Badehaus Bad Soden
· Kultur- und Festspielhaus Wittenberge

· Galerie Nupnau Art & Photographie,
  Schwaigern
· Galerie im Rathaus, Schwaigern
· Galerie Tobien, Husum
· Galerie Nottbohm, Göttingen
· Kunsthandlung Langheinz, Darmstadt

2018
· Art Karlsruhe, One-artist-show, Kunsthaus
  Lübeck
· Kulturkirche Neuruppin, *Shakespeares
  Mädchen und Frauen*, paintings and works on
  paper
· Kunsthalle Vogtland, Reichenbach
· ArtHus, Eckernförde
· Galerie Mainzer Kunst, Mainz
· Art Galerie, Siegen
· Schubertiade, Schwarzenberg / Österreich
  (in collaboration with Galerie Bode,
  Nuremberg)
· Kunstverein Peschkenhaus, Moers (with
  catalogue)
· Galerie im Alten Rathaus, Prien am Chiemsee
· Galerie Kersten, Brunnthal bei München
· Walentowski Galerie, Sylt
· Ostholstein-Museum, Eutin (Cycle: *Der wien
  Vogel fliegen kann*)
· Kunsthaus Ratingen
· Theater Wintergarten, Berlin

2019
· Städtische Galerie "Sohle 1," Bergkamen (with
  catalogue)
· Art Karlsruhe, One-artist-show, Kunsthaus
  Lübeck
· Galerie Palz, Saarlouis
· Galerie neben dem Schlesischen Museum,
  Görlitz
· Museumshof Zingst in collaboration with
  Kunstraum Wasserwerk Glowe / Rügen
· Pushkin Museum, St. Petersburg
· Galerie Richter, Lütjenburg
· Galerie Z, Landau

· Libeskind-Villa Datteln in collaboration with
  Galerie Tobien
· Schloss Britz, Berlin
· Sakralmuseum St. Annen, Kamenz
· Kulturhaus Leuna, Leuna
· Kunstraum im Gewerbepark Süd, Hilden (in
  collaboration with Geuer & Geuer Art)
· Galerie Wroblowski, Remscheid
· Kunsthalle im Bahnhof, Seebad Ahlbeck

2020
· Galerie im Lessing-Museum, Kamenz
· art + form, Dresden
· Kulturzentrum Englische Kirche Bad
  Homburg / Galerie am Dom, Wetzlar
· Artport Galerie Świnoujście / Swinemünde,
  Usedom

Editor:
Frank Thomas Gaulin, Kunsthaus Lübeck

Text:
Björn Engholm, Philipp Hontschik

Project management:
Leo Sprüth, Hatje Cantz

Production and layout:
Thomas Lemaître, Hatje Cantz

Reproductions:
Les artisants du Regard, Paris

Cover illustration:
Janis Gildein for possible.is

Copyediting:
Aaron Borgart

Translations:
Steven Lindberg (texts: Engholm, Hontschik),
Barbara Zeisl Schoenberg (texts: Mueller-Stahl)

Typeface:
Mrs Eaves XL Serif OT

Printing and binding:
Livonia Print, Riga

Paper:
Pergraphica Classic Smooth, 150 g/m²
GelTex LS, 115 g/m²

Sound engineering:
Michael Schmerschneider,
Kulturakademie Vorwerk

© 2020 Hatje Cantz Verlag, Berlin,
and authors

© 2020 for the reproduced works by Armin Mueller-Stahl:
VG Bild-Kunst, Bonn

Photographs:
Pages 8 and 11
Nicola von Velsen
Page 80
Ekkehard Nupnau

Published by:
Hatje Cantz Verlag GmbH
Mommsenstraße 27
10629 Berlin
www.hatjecantz.de
A Ganske Publishing Group Company

ISBN 978-3-7757-4723-0

Printed in Latvia

Armin Mueller-Stahl reads his poem in German, June 2020.
This QR leads to the link with the recording.